Happy Hypnosis & The 12 Steps

For Mark,
Easy does it but
D o I t !!!

❤️

Don Mon

Happy Hypnosis & The 12 Steps

AN EASIER, SOFTER WAY FOR ALL 12 STEP PROGRAMS

Don Ross

ISBN-13: 9781548069025
ISBN-10: 1548069027

Table of Contents

Prologue

A t the end of many 12 Step meetings, they join in a circle, hold hands and the leader states, "Let's have a moment of silence for the Addict who still suffers both outside and inside these rooms. Followed by the Serenity Prayer." I was one of those, in the rooms and suffering. In a perfect storm of conditions, I decided to find a way to fix it and live a happy life or end it all. Suicide is way too common among people in recovery. This book describes what I did to rewire my brain to go from suicidal on two antidepressant drugs, black out drinking, using drugs, 100 pounds overweight and smoking like a chimney to living a life that is rewarding and satisfying and reasonably happy most of the time without any medications. After a lifetime of struggling with mood disorders and emotional disturbances I have been drug free and depression free since 2010. The tools described in this book have allowed me to do that.

Introduction

f you're reading this book there is a good chance it will help you find a whole new life. One you never dreamed possible. Many of us were born into this world feeling like something was missing. In Narcotics Anonymous they say, "We were looking for something and we thought we had found it in drugs." I have heard people say they were "trying to fill a God shaped hole in their soul with anything but God." Or they may refer to "trying to find a chemical solution to a spiritual problem." Somehow or other their basic human needs were not being met and they developed dysfunctional patterns in an attempt to feel whole.

In my opinion the 12 Steps are a divinely inspired tool for change and hypnosis is the most powerful tool for personal change. Why not use them together? I have and it has saved my life. Better than that it has given me a life that exceeds my wildest dreams. Is it the only way? I don't know! It's the way that worked for me. I have seen the 12 Steps work miracles in countless lives including my own. I have seen miraculous results with hypnosis including my own. I look at hypnosis as "outside help." On page 133 of Alcoholics Anonymous the authors encourage the use of outside help, "Doctors, psychologists and practitioners of various kinds."

What I did for myself, and continue to help clients and sponsees (people I sponsor or mentor in the program) do is simply:

1) Use hypnosis to help stop the problem behavior.
2) Use the fellowship of the 12 step programs to help fill basic human needs.

3) Use the Steps to uncover the underlying issues.
4) Use hypnosis to help ameliorate or remove underlying issues and learn better coping skills.

I found myself at a point in 2009 where I recognized my life wasn't right and I needed to do something about it. I asked myself, if I'm so smart, why on earth can't I figure out how to live life happily. I had been in recovery from alcohol and drug addiction before but that didn't seem like the only problem, really it was more my solution. When I was in treatment in 1989 they told me I was "dually diagnosed." I was lucky enough to have two reasons to need help, depression, and alcoholism/drugs.

In my first recovery, I often heard people describe experiencing depressions during their recovery and digging deeper into the steps to deal with it. I thought they were wrong, I thought the Steps were okay for alcoholism but modern medical science could deal with depression. They had these new medications for that, it was a medical problem. I now, with the clarity of hindsight, think this is where I went horribly wrong. Looking back this is the fork in the road that led me to a whole other level of "bottom".

If I had followed the advice of the program, and found my way through by working the steps and other drug free modes of dealing with the depression I would have saved myself a lot of misery. I can't rewrite the past, but I can write a happy future. By sharing my experience, I hope to help others avoid the huge mistake I made.

In 1996, while in recovery, when my mother was dying of cancer, my depression worsened again and I sought help. They told me I had a chemical imbalance in my brain. Just like a diabetic needs insulin, I needed medication (SSRIs). Oh, goody I thought if I had been self-medicating my depression with drugs and alcohol, now that I had the "right stuff" doctor ordered drugs to fix my chemical imbalance.... Well then, I should now be able to resume "normal" use of drugs and alcohol, right?!?! Well that didn't work out for me. Over the course of about 10 years, I had repeated relapses or recurrences of depression while taking the meds that were supposed to fix that chemical imbalance. The answer to this apparently was increasing the dose of the SSRI and eventually adding a second one.

My drinking eventually caught up to where it had been and progressed beyond with occasional black outs. As an RN, I have always kept current with research and opinions and there were more and more negative articles surrounding SSRIs i.e. people on SSRIs had more frequent and more severe recurrences of depression. They perform no better than placebo but have negative side effects like sexual dysfunctions (depressing, right?). This caused me to want to get off them and find drug free solutions to my mood disorders. I started searching for books on depression, which led me to neuroplasticity and epigenetics. As an RN and hypnotherapist, I didn't have far to look.

That's how I found invaluable sources for training and self-hypnosis. (You can find links to them on my web site *www.HappyHypnosisSedona.com*)

While following a self-help depression program and weaning myself off the SSRIs my drinking worsened. The withdrawal from the SSRIs was worse than the depression had ever been. I probably should have been put in a hospital or something somewhere. I can vaguely remember one night going out to a local bar to broaden my social sphere as recommended by the depression recovery program. "social medicine." Well they never said not to load up on booze beforehand (okay, maybe they did I wouldn't remember anyway). I remember that night the bartender was hesitant to serve me, being fairly drunk before I got there. I'm pretty sure this is one of those "you might be an alcoholic if" sort of things. I vaguely remember the odd looks and avoidance of eye contact as I began to attempt to mingle. I did not broaden my social circles that night. I don't remember how I got home. I certainly was not in any condition to be driving, I'm glad I didn't kill anyone.

After a couple weeks of decreasing my meds and apparently increasing my drugs and alcohol my behavior had hit a point that loved ones had to sit me down. A very dear friend, my sainted Wife and a couple of others sat me down and did an intervention sort of review of my behavior over the past couple of weeks. At first I was defensive but half way through I realized She was right. "Go to AA they will love you until you can love yourself."

This was my bottom. The good thing about a bottom is everything else is better. So, this brought me back to 12 Step programs. There is much to say for hitting bottom. The more you realize that you just wouldn't want to sink any lower, the more it can feel like your choice to make a change.

Hitting Bottom

TOTAL ACCEPTANCE
He cannot picture life without alcohol.

Some day he will be unable to imagine life either with alcohol or without it.

Then he will know loneliness such as few do.

He will be at the jumping-off place.

He will wish for the end.

ALCOHOLICS ANONYMOUS, p. 152

Is there an issue in your life that is disrupting your life to this point? Or can you see that if you go on as you are, it will eventually come to this? It doesn't have to be any one substance or another. As the following list of twelve steps programs suggests, there are many ways to suffer from addiction. The 12 Steps and hypnosis can help with them all.

Take a look at the list of 12 step groups and ask yourself what is likely to pop up in my life if I don't work the steps and use hypnosis to clear away my issues!

12-Step Groups

Chemical:

Alcoholics Anonymous, Narcotics Anonymous, Methadone Support, Marijuana Anonymous, Crystal Meth Anonymous, Benzodiazepine Anonymous, Cocaine Anonymous, Smokers Anonymous, Pill Anonymous, Chemically Dependent Anonymous

Mental Health:
Mental Health Anonymous, Double Trouble Anonymous, Emotions Anonymous, Neurotics Anonymous, Dual Recovery Anonymous, Emotional Health Anonymous, Dual Diagnosis Anonymous, Schizophrenics Anonymous, Social Phobia Anonymous, Suicide Anonymous, Depressed Anonymous, Self-Harm Anonymous, Self-Mutilators Anonymous

Food:
Food Addicts in Recovery Anonymous, Food Addicts Anonymous, Overeaters Anonymous, Compulsive Eaters Anonymous, Eating Addictions Anonymous, Anorexics and Bulimics Anonymous (aba), Eating Disorders Anonymous

Money:
Online Gamers Anonymous, Gamblers Anonymous, Bettors Anonymous, Clutterers Anonymous, Debtors Anonymous, Under earners Anonymous, Workaholics Anonymous, Spenders Anonymous

General:
A.R.T.S. Anonymous, Divorce Anonymous, Fear of Success Anonymous, Nervous/Fears Recovery, Tough love Anonymous, Procrastinators Anonymous, Liars Anonymous, Conflict Anonymous, Bloggers Anonymous, All Addiction Anonymous, Recovery Anonymous, Obsessive-Compulsive Anonymous

Sexuality:
Sex Addicts Anonymous (has an email book online), Sexaholics Anonymous, Sexual Compulsives Anonymous, Sex and Love Addicts Anonymous, Sexual Recovery Anonymous, Love Addicts Anonymous, Heshe Anonymous, Homosexuals Anonymous

Medical:
Hepatitis C Anonymous, HIV AIDS Anonymous

Family:
Nar-Anon, Gam-Anon, Gam-A-Teen, Families Anonymous, Co-Anon, COSA, S-Anon, Couples in Recovery Anonymous, Co-Dependents Anonymous, Recovering Couples Anonymous, Al-Anon, Alateen, Parents Anonymous

Legal:
Kleptomaniacs and Shoplifters Anonymous, Criminal and Gangs Anonymous

Survivors:
Abuse Survivors Anonymous, Rape Survivors Anonymous, Survivors of Incest Anonymous, Trauma Anonymous, Adult Children of Alcoholics, Adult Survivors of Child Abuse Anonymous

If you know of any that have been missed here shoot me an email and I'll gladly add it to the next edition.

Addictions reside in the subconscious and per Bruce H. Lipton, Ph.D. (Author of The Biology of Belief), in an April 24, 2015 Blog on the subject there are two main ways to reshape the subconscious; hypnosis and repetition.
www.brucelipton.com/blog/there-way-change-subconscious-patterns

"Therefore, the main problem of the alcoholic centers in his mind, rather than in his body." P.23 BB

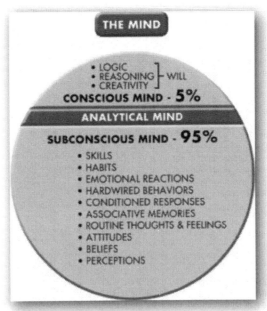

copied from You Are the Placebo by Dr Joe Dispenza.

By reading this you will learn about the 12 Steps and how hypnosis can work with them to create a "psychic change" in yourself. It will teach you to use the power of self-hypnosis while you're using the 12 Steps to recover from an addiction of any kind. Even addictions to anger, poor self-esteem, worry and anxiety. The point in writing this book is not to tell you how to do the 12 Steps. There are instructions for that in the book *Alcoholics Anonymous*, hereafter referred to as the "Big Book", or *Narcotics Anonymous* usually referred to as the "Basic Text." Other invaluable books I highly recommend are; *the Narcotics Anonymous Step Working Guides, As Bill Sees It, Twelve Steps and Twelve Traditions.*

No matter what the problem you are working on these books contain very clear and thorough instructions for using the steps to create a psychic change. A sponsor is strongly suggested to guide you through. Helping to connect the dots so to speak.

Easy Does It but Do it!!!

So how is it going so far? Are you stressed out? Having trouble absorbing what you're reading? Well, this book is designed to help with that. This would be a good time to check out the first Hypnosis written to go with this book: "Easy Does it but DO it." Designed to help soothe frazzled nerves and support the idea that you're on the right path. I have provided a recording of this free to go with the book. It can be found on my website www.HappyHypnosisSedona.com on the "Products" page.

If you haven't yet been able to stop your problem behavior but have made up your mind you'd like to, you may want to listen to "Done" or "Step 1" they are designed to help stop the addiction. All three of these are guided meditations to support you in your decision to make a change. As Dr Joe Dispenza says about his meditations "Love yourself enough to do this."

I have provided scripts for these in Appendix A. If you don't want to spend the extra money to buy the recordings you can record them in your own voice or have a trusted helper record them (use the tone, pace and rhythm of the free recording as an example). They are also available, recorded by me, for a reasonable fee on my website. *www.HappyHypnosisSedona.com*

Whatever you are going through you will feel better and be better able to absorb the information in this book after a 20-minute guided meditation. I would recommend making a habit of listening to a hypnosis recording or "guided meditation" daily as a tried and true way to improve your life.

If you to get in the habit of recognizing when you are stressed and using the tools outlined in this book to calm down. You'll notice how much better you can deal with life. I have been doing this for myself for over eight years and I am still finding my life gets better as I get better at relaxing, I get better as time goes on and the better I get, the better I get at getting better :-). Does that seem redundant?!?!?! It's a fact for me.

This is neuroplasticity, I am rewiring my mind to be more calm and peaceful. Old patterns that led to an over active fight or flight (or freeze) are rewritten to become calmer and more reasonable. This will actually down regulate some stress related DNA and up regulate other healing, restorative DNA having an actual physical impact on your health day in and day out. This is neuroplasticity and epigenetics in action. They are new sciences that are really good news to those suffering from addictions.

The physical structure of the brain changes just like the shape of your body changes as you go to the gym. Your fight or flight (or freeze) center in your brain (the amygdala) has been shown to become smaller after just eight weeks of a mindfulness meditation practice. Self-hypnosis (listening to guided meditations/hypnosis recordings) qualifies as a mindfulness practice.

http://news.harvard.edu/gazette/story/2011/01/eight-weeks-to-a-better-brain/

This has a huge impact on your overall health, mental and physical. Dr Bruce Lipton, Ph.D. (author of *Biology of Belief*) *has* said 90% of disease stems from fear or stress through overuse of this fight or fight (or freeze) mechanism. I believe this is true.

Subconscious patterns can cause this fight or flight (or freeze) response to be fired off way more than is healthy. In the case of an emergency the amygdala takes control. It is in the limbic system, the most primitive part of our brains. The amygdala is not able to distinguish between a real or imagined threat and will become boss; issuing orders on how to behave, initiating the fight or flight (or freeze) response. This process suspends or slows down all non-essential bodily functions (e.g. digestion and immune system functioning) and inhibits rational thinking. You can appreciate how repeated firing of it could affect your health and relationships. I think of these subconscious patterns as logs in the fire that fuel your need for escape leading to addictions.

Feelings of Irritability, restlessness, and discontent leading to avoidant escapist behavior

Stress
Flight or Fight or Freeze

Underlying Issues

Possible underlying issues are anything that causes your basic human needs not to be met. Could be PTSD, past life issues, childhood trauma, genetic traumatic memories, negative thinking styles...what are your logs under the fire?

Hypnosis and mindfulness practices can rewire the brain to be relaxed much more of the time. When you practice mindfulness and become aware of when you are stressed you can use hypnosis and the other tools described in chapter 3 to train the brain to be relaxed more of the time. While using hypnosis to rewire subconscious patterns that are unnecessarily setting off your fight or flight (or freeze).

I found using self-hypnosis concurrently with the 12 Steps to be very helpful. On page 133 of the book Alcoholics Anonymous it states: "God has abundantly supplied this world with fine doctors, psychologists, and practitioners of various kinds. Do not hesitate to take your health problems to such persons." I consider using self-hypnosis as coming under this area. Helping to quiet our minds to enable us to process what we're doing while we're doing the Steps is what hypnosis has done for me and many of my clients. Nowhere does it say not to find outside help with quieting our frazzled nerves as we use the Steps to clear away the wreckage of the past. Hypnosis is a proven tool for creating change on a subconscious level. That is also what the 12 Steps will do.

I have used both hypnosis and repetition along with daily mindfulness practice (as in listening to a guided meditation/hypnosis download recording daily). In 12-Step Programs we repeat many things over and over. There are several readings usually at the beginning and end of most meetings. Step 11's emphasis on meditation in addition to prayer certainly leaves room for consideration of hypnosis. There are many examples of what I recognize as hypnotic techniques in the literature.

Using hypnosis and 12-Step programs together to enhance each other is incredibly powerful and if you do what I did you will experience a huge change in your outlook on life and the world you live in. The goal of recovery is to lead a HAPPY JOYOUS AND FREE life. I believe that every last one of us is capable of that.

No matter what your past is like you can use the steps to help "clear away the wreckage of the past." As it says in the 9th Step promises, "We do not regret the past nor wish to shut the door on it." BB p 84.

Many people are prescribed medications by well-meaning practitioners and I won't debate that issue here. For me that ended in disaster twice! If you take away the pain with medication you take away the motivation to change. "Pain is the touchstone of all spiritual growth."

Again, my experience, take it for what it's worth. Some very smart people believe there is no sense to psychopharmacology. Drugs don't change neuropathways, they slow them down. Advances in neuroscience have led to the understanding of neuroplasticity. And the new science of epigenetics shows us we can determine how our genetics are expressed. We are not doomed to live out what we inherited from our parents.

My belief and experience as a hypnotherapist is that no matter what the brain may be doing wrong it can be rewired to do it right. That has been my experience for myself and the hundreds of clients I have helped. I have found that using a recording at least once a day has really helped calm my overactive fight or flight response, allowing me to see things more clearly and therefore to better do the 12 Steps. In addition to the recordings I have written for this book, I highly recommend the recordings from online that I used daily. I still use them and I often use the scripts they offer with many of my clients. I have included a link to them on my site *www.HappyHypnosisSedona.com* at the bottom of the page "about Don". There is also a link to much of the training that I have used and recommend. There's a convenient link halfway down the page "about Don" if you are interested in exploring hypnosis training.

On bad days, I listened to the recordings several times. I always felt better afterward. I'm sure I was experiencing what they call "post-acute withdrawal syndrome" in addition to the withdrawal from the antidepressant drugs I had probably weaned myself from too abruptly. For months, I was extremely anxious. I made myself attend meetings but while I was there I was so anxious my shirt would stick to my back from nervous perspiration.

I hope you're not in as bad a shape as I was but however bad off you are please be assured it will get better. If you are planning to hurt yourself or someone else tell someone, get help with it. It will get better. If you "Google" "suicide helpline" there are many options available to you. Don't make a permanent solution for problems that are temporary.

National Suicide Prevention Lifeline (USA)

Call 1-800-273-8255

There is excellent information on depression including suicide hotline numbers at *www.clinical-depression.co.uk/?6874* You are not alone!!! My Sponsor, Ray, says we (in recovery) are a mixed bag of nuts. We (12-Step programs) have a wrench for every nut. Take what seems to fit you and don't worry about the rest. Easy does it. .....but do it.

Everyone I have ever seen go through a 12-Step program has benefited immensely. "Rarely have we seen a person fail who has thoroughly followed our path."

I don't intend this book to be proof of anything. There is plenty of research demonstrating the efficacy of hypnosis and the 12 Steps. I only want to describe the huge change in my life I experienced and have seen in others using hypnosis and/or the 12 Steps. I have also seen many who have only used one or the other with not that great of results. I live in a fairly small community yet every year or two someone in the program, well known and apparently actively "working" the program commits or attempts suicide.

Also, I see far too many get caught up in a revolving door, in and out over and over. It is frustrating to me to see this and know there but for the Grace of my Higher Power go I. I had been studying and practicing hypnosis for eight years before I found myself in the trouble I described above. I really don't know how I would have done with just the steps or just the hypnosis.

If you are unsure that is okay with me, I have seen much more thorough results with those with a healthy skepticism. Try it for yourself. What have you got to lose?

If you do what I did, use hypnosis to help quit. Allow the fellowship to help fill your basic human needs. Then as you continue to uncover your underlying issues by "working" the Steps you can use hypnosis to ameliorate them. Repeat this until you are self-actualized or dead. That's my plan and so far, it is working great.

CHAPTER 1

Hypnosis? Really?

Yes really, *Washington Times April 28, 2013-*
"Hypnosis seems helpful in treating addictions and
the depression and anxiety associated with them"
- PSYCHOLOGY TODAY

When you think of hypnosis you likely think of quitting smoking, right? Most people know or have heard of someone who has used hypnosis to quit smoking. The first things they taught us in my hypnosis training was smoking cessation and weight loss. When you think of it, that's really a testament to the efficacy of hypnosis and it's use for deep rooted addictions. Smoking can be one of the hardest if not THE hardest addiction to break.

Research shows hypnosis to be over 3 times more effective than nicotine replacement therapy and15 times more effective than quitting cold turkey.

www.yourbettertomorrow.com/easiest-way-to-stop-smoking

Even after a persuasive mid-nineties reanalysis of 18 hypnotic studies showed that psychotherapy clients who learned self-hypnosis lost twice as much weight as those who didn't (and, in one study, kept it off two years after treatment ended), hypnotherapy has remained a well-kept weight loss secret.

http://www.oprah.com/health/hypnosis-for-weight-loss-can-hypnosis-help-you-lose-weight

Smoking is a habit, right? A subconscious pattern that has been wired into a person's behavior. Every time they smoke they associate it with a reward. Like Pavlov's dog salivating when he hears a bell ring, the smoker automatically lights up at certain triggers. The phone rings, have a cup of coffee, finish a meal, have good sex, have bad sex, the sun comes up. There are thousands of triggers that can get wired into the persons smoking habit. I have been trained to help the smoker recognize the trigger using metacognition. Then when triggered to use what we call pattern collapse to rewire our response. "Just rub your thumb against your finger and imagine that urge to smoke getting smaller and smaller, weaker and weaker." Then each and every time they don't follow through with the subconscious pattern (pattern collapse) it gets weaker (neuroplasticity-pruning) Rehearsing this in a hypnotic state helps to erase old patterns and write successful ones. Why not do the same thing with any habit, addiction, or problem behavior? Continuously looking for faulty programming that can be rewired to helpful patterns.

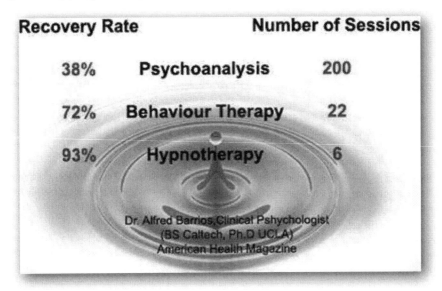

Recovery Rate		Number of Sessions
38%	Psychoanalysis	200
72%	Behaviour Therapy	22
93%	Hypnotherapy	6

Dr. Alfred Barrios, Clinical Pshychologist
(BS Caltech, Ph.D UCLA)
American Health Magazine

So how does hypnosis work? There are many books on this topic. There are differing schools of thought. For our purposes let's keep it simple. There is an induction that leads you in to an altered brain state, usually alpha. It's a choice you make to follow along. Then deepeners are used to bring you into theta brain waves where real change occurs rapidly and efficiently. It's like pushing the "record" button on a tape recorder. You can erase old patterns and record new ones.

At this point you can address the issue or problem behavior, a negative thinking pattern, or old "tape" you want to rewrite. What is it you want to accomplish, what do you want to change? We're looking for faulty programming that can be rewired. You can address anything, from just becoming someone who spends less time worrying to changing an addiction from something you can't stop to something you used to do but that just doesn't appeal anymore. Take a log out of the fire that drives your need to escape and pour water on it.

Again, this book isn't intended to teach you everything there is to know about hypnosis. There are hundreds of great books for that and several schools of thought. I found it really helped me work my way through the 12 Steps. My training is described on my website *www.HappyHypnosSedona.com* "about Don". I've included a link to some of the training I took halfway down the page.

In addition to using it to help stop drinking alcohol I personally have used it for all kinds of things. I lost over 100 pounds, quit smoking, quit thinking negatively. I've used it to relieve pain, hay fever and clear up eczema. The mind is way more powerful than most of us realize. Whenever I recognize a problem I ask myself if there is a faulty program that can be rewired? If the answer is yes I look for a hypnosis to help change it. The hypnosis I wrote for steps 6&7 is very good for this.

In the book *Heal Yourself with Medical Hypnosis* Dr Andrew Weil and Steve Gurgevich Ph.D. do a great job describing how major medical journals are finally beginning to recognize hypnosis as a legitimate clinical tool, citing proof positive that it can help ease chronic pain, lessen the side effects of chemotherapy, counteract anxiety and sleep disorders, and more. One eye opening example they describe is a six-year-old girl with warts on her vocal chords. Removing them by an ENT failed to prevent them with the warts recurring. When addressed with hypnosis "pretend you are little enough to go into your own throat and chop away at the warts." They cleared up and didn't return. The mind has much more influence on the body than most of us ever imagined, including myself.

Another eye-opening study I came across was *www.IBShypnosis.com* Dr. Olafur Palson a gastroenterologist has performed a study at the University of North Carolina. Hypnosis far outperformed counseling and placebo pills in reducing symptoms of pain and bloating in patients with severe Irritable Bowel Syndrome.

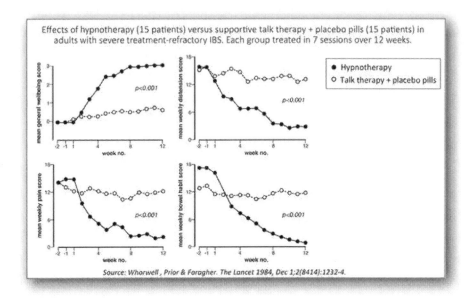

Effects of hypnotherapy (15 patients) versus supportive talk therapy + placebo pills (15 patients) in adults with severe treatment-refractory IBS. Each group treated in 7 sessions over 12 weeks.

Source: Whorwell, Prior & Faragher. The Lancet 1984, Dec 1;2(8414):1232-4.

When people quit an addiction cold turkey they go through a period of withdrawal. The trigger occurs, they consciously resist it, which causes some amount of stress. If, however the stress of resisting the trigger is too great they often give in and resume the behavior feeling worse about themselves (adding logs to that fire).

In hypnosis, we actually get into that pattern and like pushing the record button on a tape recorder we record over the old response to the trigger with a new response. "see yourself rubbing your finger against your thumb and feeling that urge to smoke get weaker and weaker." Rubbing the finger on the thumb can eventually become the "default" response to the "trigger" that formerly resulted in an almost undeniable response of smoking. The benefits of hypnosis are long lasting. I have heard people who quit "cold turkey" still reporting urges to smoke 15 years after quitting. When you rewire the trigger as I described above you may eventually not even think of smoking. I have one client that reported being asked something about when they smoked and replying, "I never smoked" that's how well she had erased it from her subconscious. We had strengthened the part of her that wouldn't smoke and weakened the part that did for fifty years.

Addictions reside in the subconscious and those who know, like Dr Bruce Lipton, Ph.D. (Author of The Biology of Belief), know, there are two main ways to reshape the subconscious; hypnosis and repetition. "Therefore, the main problem of the alcoholic centers in his mind, rather than in his body." Alcoholics' Anonymous P.23 BB

THE MIND

- LOGIC
- REASONING ⎤ WILL
- CREATIVITY ⎦

CONSCIOUS MIND - 5%

ANALYTICAL MIND

SUBCONSCIOUS MIND - 95%

- SKILLS
- HABITS
- EMOTIONAL REACTIONS
- HARDWIRED BEHAVIORS
- CONDITIONED RESPONSES
- ASSOCIATIVE MEMORIES
- ROUTINE THOUGHTS & FEELINGS
- ATTITUDES
- BELIEFS
- PERCEPTIONS

Feelings of irritability, restlessness, and discontent leading to avoidant escapist behavior

Stress
Flight or Fight or Freeze

Underlying Issues

Possible underlying issues are anything that causes your basic human needs not to be met. Could be PTSD, past life issues, childhood trauma, genetic traumatic memories, negative thinking styles...what are your logs under the fire?

"Maybe you are searching among the branches, for what only appears in the roots."-Rumi

I found for myself all these possible logs in the fire existed and my overall feeling of peace (comfortable in my own skin) improved as I used hypnosis and the 12 steps to clear them up. These are the source of the faulty programming.

You may notice I included things in the list of potential "logs" that may not be accepted scientific fact. Oh well, what can I say. I have experienced these things, like past life regression. Whether they're real or not I couldn't be sure. I know that exploring it with hypnosis had a beneficial effect on me.

Another issue that is more recently described is genetic stress disorder. A phrase I may have made up. It describes my experience again. There have been some recent articles describing experiments with mice. Not very kind to the mouse but apparently, they would introduce a certain smell (cherry blossom I think) then give the poor defenseless rodent an electrical shock. After repeating this several times the mouse would react with panic behavior when only the smell was introduced. No shock necessary. Well this isn't that surprising, is it? Much like the work of Pavlov and his more humane treatment of the drooling dog. The surprising part, and the part that gave me a huge "aha", was that the offspring of the mouse without ever being subject to, or even witness to the shocking, would react with the same panic type behavior when exposed to the smell. Apparently, this carried through to the next generation as well.

This resounded with me as I have been aware that my father suffered PTSD from his experiences in WWII. He was one of the 101st Airborne who liberated the Dachau concentration camp. I never knew him as he died of cancer at age 37 (I was seven) but I heard stories of him waking in the night screaming from nightmares related to his experiences there.

I believe I inherited some of his terror and guilt from those events. It explains why I have never felt "comfortable in my own skin." I guess it makes sense for the offspring of people living through terror to have heightened fight or flight (or freeze) response. They are then better prepared for life in a war zone. Not better prepared to live a calm peaceful happy life but to survive in dangerous conditions.

Hypnosis has helped me rewire problem programming, to practice mindfulness to separate legitimate emotions from these inherited ones. Eckhart Tolle in his book The *Power of Now*, talks about healing your "pain body" these are the things that contributed to my addiction, the logs in my fire. There are many tools to help with this. For me Hypnosis and the 12 Steps were the most powerful. I'll describe some others in chapter 3 other tools.

Some schools of thought would describe addiction itself as a disease. Perhaps a genetic disease that your genes determine from birth. I have heard there are presently 15 genes implicated in depression. For me as for many, depression is closely related to my addictions. But the recent revelations of epigenetics tell us that these genes can all be expressed thousands of different ways. That leads me to believe that our environments have led us to subconscious patterns that lead to negative thinking styles, dysfunctional relationships and a failure to adequately meet our basic needs. This is what leads us to feel like outsiders and fall prey to habitual escaping behaviors that lead to chemical dependencies and thrill seeking.

I think the disease model has its advantages, it allows us to remove the shame "log" from our fire. My addiction/mental health problem isn't my fault it's a disease. This is great but if it leads you to think there is nothing that can be done about it, that's not so good. I think it's more accurate that we are programmed by our parents. Hypnosis can change that subconscious programming.

Whatever is causing you to feel a need to escape can be rewired with hypnosis and neuroplasticity to feelings of safety and self-esteem (start doing estimable things). Following the 12 Steps helps to develop a grateful altruistic attitude.

If you don't reduce the stress that the addiction is helping to cope with (remove some logs from the fire) you are likely to find other unhealthy behaviors to deal with the underlying stress and the increased stress of fighting the triggers. This often leads to a sort of "Whack-a- Mole" game of addictions. I think the following is worth repeating.

Take a look at the list of 12 step groups and ask yourself what is likely to pop up in my life if I don't work the steps and use hypnosis to clear away my issues!

12-Step Groups

Chemical:
Alcoholics Anonymous, Narcotics Anonymous, Methadone Support, Marijuana Anonymous, Crystal Meth Anonymous, Benzodiazepine Anonymous, Cocaine Anonymous, Smokers Anonymous, Pill Anonymous, Chemically Dependent Anonymous

Mental Health:
Mental Health Anonymous, Double Trouble Anonymous, Emotions Anonymous, Neurotics Anonymous, Dual Recovery Anonymous, Emotional Health Anonymous, Dual Diagnosis Anonymous, Schizophrenics Anonymous, Social Phobia Anonymous, Suicide Anonymous, Depressed Anonymous, Self-Harm Anonymous, Self-Mutilators Anonymous

Food:
Food Addicts in Recovery Anonymous, Food Addicts Anonymous, Overeaters Anonymous, Compulsive Eaters Anonymous, Eating Addictions Anonymous, Anorexics and Bulimics Anonymous (aba), Eating Disorders Anonymous

Money:
Online Gamers Anonymous, Gamblers Anonymous, Bettors Anonymous, Clutterers Anonymous, Debtors Anonymous, Under earners Anonymous, Workaholics Anonymous, Spenders Anonymous

General:
A.R.T.S. Anonymous, Divorce Anonymous, Fear of Success Anonymous, Nervous/Fears Recovery, Tough love Anonymous, Procrastinators Anonymous, Liars Anonymous, Conflict Anonymous, Bloggers Anonymous, All Addiction Anonymous, Recovery Anonymous, Obsessive-Compulsive Anonymous

Sexuality:
Sex Addicts Anonymous (has an email book online), Sexaholics Anonymous, Sexual Compulsives Anonymous, Sex and Love Addicts Anonymous, Sexual Recovery Anonymous, Love Addicts Anonymous, Heshe Anonymous, Homosexuals Anonymous

Medical:
Hepatitis C Anonymous, HIV AIDS Anonymous

Family:
Nar-Anon, Gam-Anon, Gam-A-Teen, Families Anonymous, Co-Anon, COSA, S-Anon, Couples in Recovery Anonymous, Co-Dependents Anonymous, Recovering Couples Anonymous, Al-Anon, Alateen, Parents Anonymous

Legal:
Kleptomaniacs and Shoplifters Anonymous, Criminal and Gangs Anonymous

Survivors:
Abuse Survivors Anonymous, Rape Survivors Anonymous, Survivors of Incest Anonymous, Trauma Anonymous, Adult Children of Alcoholics, Adult Survivors of Child Abuse Anonymous

Between the 12 Steps and self-hypnosis I have rewired my brain for a whole new experience of life. I have shown many clients how to do the same and I guarantee you; if you do what I did you can have what I have, a life that's reasonably happy most of the time.

Maybe you're a person involved in helping others and want to know something about the use of self-hypnosis and the 12 Steps. That's good too. ☺ I'm talking about miraculous changes and to achieve this you must open your mind to the possibility that miracles can occur in your life. Many have been denied miraculous change due to a closed mind. The idea that your genes determine everything has caused so many of us to accept being broken in such a way that only pills can fix us. Thanks to the new sciences of epigenetics and neuroplasticity I have found I don't have to be doomed to cancer because both my parents had it. Neither do I have to suffer depression and addictions just because it "runs" in my family. Those genes are just blueprints and I can influence how they are interpreted. The work of Bruce Lipton Ph.D. (author of the Biology of Belief) clearly shows this to be true. I highly recommend following his teaching.

The following is a good start toward having an open mind. You may want to start a practice of repeating this simple prayer each time you read this book or do other work on your problems. (repetition)

Set Aside Prayer

God, help me to set aside everything I think I know about myself, my disease, this program and especially You, so that I can have an open mind and a new experience with all these things. God, help me to see the truth.

Have you guys ever heard about the Paranoids Anonymous groups????? Me neither, they won't tell anyone where they meet!

CHAPTER 2

So, What's the Deal with These Steps

"A journey of a thousand miles begins with a single step."
– Lao Tzu

Working the steps will help you uncover faulty programming, logs on your fire, that are driving your addiction. My experience, strength and hope may be useful to you, it may ring true to you or it may not. There are a million variations on addiction and mine is just one of them. All can benefit from learning and using the Steps. There are quite a few groups that have adopted and adapted the original 12 Steps developed by the founders of AA. Let's take another look at the list of 12 Step programs. As I look through them I can see I could probably qualify for and benefit from several of them, most of us could. For myself I have found one program that fills my needs. I have heard many others that attend meetings in more than one. Like going to AA and CA. Or AA and Alanon.

Either way is fine if you recognize that just stopping one harmful behavior without addressing thoroughly the underlying issues will only   result in other problem behaviors arising. The previously mentioned addictions "Wack-a-Mole " game.

12-Step Groups

Chemical:
Alcoholics Anonymous, Narcotics Anonymous, Methadone Support, Marijuana Anonymous, Crystal Meth Anonymous, Benzodiazepine Anonymous,

Cocaine Anonymous, Smokers Anonymous, Pill Anonymous, Chemically Dependent Anonymous

Mental Health:
Mental Health Anonymous, Double Trouble Anonymous, Emotions Anonymous, Neurotics Anonymous, Dual Recovery Anonymous, Emotional Health Anonymous, Dual Diagnosis Anonymous, Schizophrenics Anonymous, Social Phobia Anonymous, Suicide Anonymous, Depressed Anonymous, Self Harm Anonymous, Self Mutilators Anonymous

Food:
Food Addicts in Recovery Anonymous, Food Addicts Anonymous, Overeaters Anonymous, Compulsive Eaters Anonymous, Eating Addictions Anonymous, Anorexics and Bulimics Anonymous (aba), Eating Disorders Anonymous

Money:
Online Gamers Anonymous, Gamblers Anonymous, Bettors Anonymous, Clutterers Anonymous, Debtors Anonymous, Under earners Anonymous, Workaholics Anonymous, Spenders Anonymous

General:
A.R.T.S. Anonymous, Divorce Anonymous, Fear of Success Anonymous, Nervous/Fears Recovery, Tough love Anonymous, Procrastinators Anonymous, Liars Anonymous, Conflict Anonymous, Bloggers Anonymous, All Addiction Anonymous, Recovery Anonymous, Obsessive-Compulsive Anonymous

Sexuality:
Sex Addicts Anonymous (has an email book online), Sexaholics Anonymous, Sexual Compulsives Anonymous, Sex and Love Addicts Anonymous, Sexual Recovery Anonymous, Love Addicts Anonymous, Heshe Anonymous, Homosexuals Anonymous

Medical:
Hepatitis C Anonymous, HIV AIDS Anonymous

Family:
Nar-Anon, Gam-Anon, Gam-A-Teen, Families Anonymous, Co-Anon, COSA, S-Anon, Couples in Recovery Anonymous, Co-Dependents Anonymous, Recovering Couples Anonymous, Al-Anon, Alateen, Parents Anonymous

Legal:
Kleptomaniacs and Shoplifters Anonymous, Criminal and Gangs Anonymous

Survivors:
Abuse Survivors Anonymous, Rape Survivors Anonymous, Survivors of Incest Anonymous, Trauma Anonymous, Adult Children of Alcoholics, Adult Survivors of Child Abuse Anonymous

Take a look at the list of 12 step groups and ask yourself what is likely to pop up in my life if I don't work the steps and use hypnosis to clear away my issues!

The founders of AA, Bill W. and Dr Bob originally created the Twelve steps. They were adapted from Six steps used by the Oxford Group. I have included some background in appendix B and some alternative forms of the steps in appendix C. The heart of the suggested program of personal recovery is contained in Twelve Steps describing the experience of the earliest members of the Society:

1. We admitted we were powerless over alcohol—that our lives had become unmanageable.
2. Came to believe that a Power greater than ourselves could restore us to sanity.
3. Made a decision to turn our will and our lives over to the care of God *as we understood Him.*
4. Made a searching and fearless moral inventory of ourselves.
5. Admitted to God, to ourselves, and to another human being the exact nature of our wrongs.
6. Were entirely ready to have God remove all these defects of character.
7. Humbly asked Him to remove our shortcomings.
8. Made a list of all persons we had harmed, and became willing to make amends to them all.
9. Made direct amends to such people wherever possible, except when to do so would injure them or others.
10. Continued to take personal inventory and when we were wrong promptly admitted it.
11. Sought through prayer and meditation to improve our conscious contact with God *as we understood Him,* praying only for knowledge of His will for us and the power to carry that out.
12. Having had a spiritual awakening as the result of these steps, we tried to carry this message to alcoholics and to practice these principles in all our affairs.

These have been adopted and adapted with permission by the many groups listed above. I like to look at them as a tried and true formula for clearing away the mess of your addiction and the underlying issues that led to it. I described it to one sponsee (someone I am "sponsoring" or mentoring through the steps), Mike, as sort of like going through their cluttered garage getting ready for a garage sale because they couldn't any longer park their car in there. It's a way of sorting through your dysfunctional life, finding what doesn't work and what does.

Steps 1-3 waking up, Steps 4-6 cleaning up, Steps 7-9 making up, Steps 10-12 keeping it up - Anonymous

Here is the version used by NA with a brief description of the purpose of each step.

Narcotics Anonymous 12 Steps to Recovery *(with a brief description included italics added)*

1. We admitted that we were powerless over our addiction; that our lives had become unmanageable.
    When you see the disasters your addiction has caused and acknowledge your real need for help, you face reality with humility and open the door for a changed life.

2. We came to believe that a Power greater than ourselves could restore us to sanity.
    You learn that your life can turn from hopeless to hopeful - because there is a stronger Power outside of yourself that is able to piece your life back together and renew you. You have the personal choice to decide what or who that Higher Power is for you.

3. We made a decision to turn our will and our lives over to the care of God as we understood Him.
    Your heart, mind and will take action by surrendering to this Higher Power. You trust that this Higher Power will guide your behaviors with better wisdom and care than you can do by yourself.

4. We made a searching and fearless moral inventory of ourselves.
    As you gently try to peel away the many layers of your being and better understand your depths, you allow yourself to experience a much fuller healing, restoration and freedom.

5. We admitted to God, to ourselves, and to another human being the exact nature of our wrongs.
    Now that you've more closely examined yourself, you gather your courage and confess - to yourself, to others and to your Higher Power - the darkness that you find inside yourself. By admitting what you've been

previously hiding, you can better accept yourself and make changes in your relationships.

6. We were entirely ready to have God remove all these defects of character.
   By working through your fears and uncertainties about becoming a better person and making the changes you need to make in your life, you prepare yourself to invite your Higher Power to change you.

7. We humbly asked Him to remove our shortcomings.
   As you ask your Higher Power to remove your character flaws, you also take actions that give your Higher Power greater ability to work changes into your life.

8. We made a list of all persons we had harmed, and became willing to make amends to them all.
   Here, you assess all the ways you could have possibly caused harm to others and also to yourself. You then make yourself ready to restore these relationships through both words and actions.

9. We made direct amends to such people wherever possible, except when to do so would injure them or others.
   First, you need to face your fears and expectations in making these amends; you try to forgive anyone who needs your forgiveness and you sensitively evaluate where making amends would do more harm than good. You then take the risk of feeling vulnerable and make amends to these individuals.

10. We continued to take personal inventory and when we were wrong promptly admitted it.
    You make it a habit to reassess yourself for any future wrongs you may commit as you strive towards better behavior, and you confess your wrongs as soon as you become aware of them.

11. We sought through prayer and meditation to improve our conscious contact with God as we understood Him, praying only for knowledge of His will for us and the power to carry that out.

In this step, you continue to increase your reliance on your Higher Power as your source of guidance and as your strength to walk according to this guidance.

12. Having had a spiritual awakening as the result of these steps, we tried to carry this message to addicts, and to practice these principles in all our affairs.
By this point in the Narcotics Anonymous 12 steps, you have renewed yourself through your unique spiritual pathway, having found genuine hope in being able to stay clean and recover. You aim to both continue this pathway, yourself, and also share your journey and hope with others.[2]

copiedfrom:http://www.recovery.org/topics/about-the-narcotics-anonymous-na-12-step-recovery-program/

Between the wreckage our addiction has created and our underlying issues, which caused the addiction in the first place, we have a tangled mess. We can't straighten it out all at once. If we clear away the worst first, with steps 4 and 5, we can then get to the underlying issues with steps 6 and 7. With the help of hypnosis we systematically take the logs out of the fire first and find peace.

12 Steps for Laundry

For some reason, I thought of this version while talking with a female spon-see, Michelle. We both enjoyed it and it helps make clear the functionality of the steps. It's a tool we can use over and over. Once we get the hang of it, it becomes automatic for us.

1. These clothes are really dirty. I can't wear them and I don't want to go nudist.
2. I have heard of a machine that can fix this it's the washer and dryer.
3. I have decided to do a load of laundry.
4. I throw them in the washer. Okay I also sort them first, ones I will tear up for rags, ones I will give to Goodwill, ones that go in the yard sale and ones I still like and will wear.
5. I throw them in the dryer. Or hang them on the line.
6. I don't want to just leave them in a tangled mess in the basket.
7. I fold them and pile them up nicely.
8. I decide some need ironing and put them aside.
9. I iron the ones that the label says can be ironed. I don't iron the ones that would be screwed worse by the ironing.
10. I try to take care of my clothes better. I realize if I roll around on the floor I will have to do laundry sooner.
11. I look at what clothes look good on me and make myself look nice.
12. I encourage others to take pride in their appearance and give good fashion tips when I can.

So why do the 12 Steps, what's the purpose. You may have heard that a person has to hit bottom before they can recover. I have found there's always flexibility and semantics involved with all the aspects of using the Steps for change in varying degrees. An early sponsor of mine (I have had several) said "basically there has to be a problem you haven't been able to fix that's causing you enough pain that you're willing to do the Steps".

People talk about the "Gift of Desperation." I feel the more resistant to change your problem has been, the more difficulty this problem has caused you, the more completely you will be willing to commit yourself to the process of change (working the Steps). It's negotiable and can be amended as you go along. I have seen alcoholics (including myself) continue drinking in spite of horrible health consequences. They seem to be blind to the damage it's doing "in denial." This is true for any addictive activity. Until they see it as a problem that must be fixed, until they "hit bottom," they won't change. So, Step 1: "We admitted we were powerless over _____ and our lives were unmanageable." We seemed to be in a cycle of behavior that had become a hell instead of fun. The party is over but we're still chasing that lost high.

The first word of the first step is very important "We." It's a "We" program. You're not going to want to read books by yourself and think you're going to get better. Some of the most current thinking on addictions is that it is stemming from separation rather than genetics. Getting better involves being part of the human race and if you have a problem of this nature you have probably allowed it to separate you from being a member of the family of man. That is what I was trying to do at that bar. The recovery from depression program I followed (link available on my website *www.HappyHypnosisSedona.com*). Shows how "social medicine "is vital to our filling our basic needs as outlined by the "Human Givens" The nine basic human needs are as follows.

1. The need to give and receive attention
2. Taking heed of the mind body connection
3. The need for purpose, goals and meaning
4. A sense of community and making a contribution
5. The need for challenge and creativity
6. The need for intimacy
7. The need to feel a sense of control
8. The need for a sense of status
9. The need for a sense safety and security

If these basic needs aren't met trouble arises. I think the Human Givens propose that all mental issues stem from these needs not being met.

Much of these needs are met by attending meetings and being involved in 12 Step groups.

When I was drinking, I could step into most bars and find companionship and status etc. just by buying a round of drinks. Until my drinking got to the point where bartenders didn't want to serve me and I was drinking to oblivion at home. Now, thanks to 12 Step programs, anywhere I go I can find a group of people who will instantly accept me as one of them. There are all kinds of 12 Step meetings all over the world. Open meetings allow anyone to attend so you don't have to feel like you're not welcome at an NA meeting if you only drank alcohol. A drug is a drug and alcohol certainly is. At an "Open meeting" you don't have to say or do anything.

You need to find your "Tribe." Most people suffering from addictions have become isolated. Your basic human needs are no longer met in healthy ways. You need "social medicine" as I learned in the depression self-help course.

If your problem is drink, go to AA. If it's gambling, go to GA. Shop around. There are all kinds of groups, take another look at the list.

12-Step Groups

Chemical:
Alcoholics Anonymous, Narcotics Anonymous, Methadone Support, Marijuana Anonymous, Crystal Meth Anonymous, Benzodiazepine Anonymous, Cocaine Anonymous, Smokers Anonymous, Pill Anonymous, Chemically Dependent Anonymous

Mental Health:
Mental Health Anonymous, Double Trouble Anonymous, Emotions Anonymous, Neurotics Anonymous, Dual Recovery Anonymous, Emotional Health Anonymous, Dual Diagnosis Anonymous, Schizophrenics Anonymous, Social Phobia Anonymous, Suicide Anonymous, Depressed Anonymous, Self-Harm Anonymous, Self-Mutilators Anonymous

Food:
Food Addicts in Recovery Anonymous, Food Addicts Anonymous, Overeaters Anonymous, Compulsive Eaters Anonymous, Eating Addictions Anonymous, Anorexics and Bulimics Anonymous (aba), Eating Disorders Anonymous

Money:
Online Gamers Anonymous, Gamblers Anonymous, Bettors Anonymous, Clutterers Anonymous, Debtors Anonymous, Under earners Anonymous, Workaholics Anonymous, Spenders Anonymous

General:
A.R.T.S. Anonymous, Divorce Anonymous, Fear of Success Anonymous, Nervous/Fears Recovery, Tough love Anonymous, Procrastinators Anonymous, Liars Anonymous, Conflict Anonymous, Bloggers Anonymous, All Addiction Anonymous, Recovery Anonymous, Obsessive-Compulsive Anonymous

Sexuality:
Sex Addicts Anonymous (has an email book online), Sexaholics Anonymous, Sexual Compulsives Anonymous, Sex and Love Addicts Anonymous, Sexual Recovery Anonymous, Love Addicts Anonymous, Heshe Anonymous, Homosexuals Anonymous

Medical:
Hepatitis C Anonymous, HIV AIDS Anonymous

Family:
Nar-Anon, Gam-Anon, Gam-A-Teen, Families Anonymous, Co-Anon, COSA, S-Anon, Couples in Recovery Anonymous, Co-Dependents Anonymous, Recovering Couples Anonymous, Al-Anon, Alateen, Parents Anonymous

Legal:
Kleptomaniacs and Shoplifters Anonymous, Criminal, and Gangs Anonymous

Survivors:
Abuse Survivors Anonymous, Rape Survivors Anonymous, Survivors of Incest Anonymous, Trauma Anonymous, Adult Children of Alcoholics, Adult Survivors of Child Abuse Anonymous

Women's only, Men's only, The Rainbow Club, Bikers, Bible People, Atheists. I recommend a plain old everyday meeting. Look for "open meetings" – "anyone is welcome to attend" Here in Sedona, AZ there are a fairly diverse offering of groups with 4-6 meetings on any given day. Some remote areas may have fewer. A Google search will help you find your area's offerings. You will find acceptance and companionship and you will see the miracle of recovery in others. "It works-it really does."

If for some reason, you are unable to connect with fellow sufferers in person there are online versions of all sorts of 12 Step programs. I have used "In the Rooms" when unable to get to a face to face meeting.

You may go through all 12 Steps in 48 hours or take a year to do Step 1. It's not a one size fits all thing. Again, the right sponsor will help with this. No one thinks a cookie cutter program is going to fix everyone. Lately there is talk that AA is only 5-10% effective. I'm pretty sure it works if you work it. " Rarely have we seen a person fail who has thoroughly followed our path." I've never seen anyone not benefit from doing this work.

Even if you rush through the Steps you will benefit from it. You may then do it again more thoroughly and benefit from that. Each time you go through the Steps you see things more clearly, you get a new pair of glasses. You're uncovering problem programming and reprogramming it. You eventually get to a point where it becomes automatic.

At one beginner's meeting I attend the leader reads the following advice each week "Some of our long-time members suggest the following; get a sponsor or temporary sponsor right away, get a Big Book and read it, get lots of phone numbers and use them, get to a meeting every day for 90 days and don't drink in between. Whatever you do keep coming back."

CHAPTER 3

Other Tools

n addition to hypnosis there are some other tools I have used and teach my clients and sponsees to use to dispel negative emotions. These include "Ho 'O Ponopono", Faster EFT, Laughing Yoga, and breath work. You can "Google" these and search for YouTube videos to explain them. There are tons of good resources on them. They are very helpful as you deal with the emotions that come up as you work through your issues.

Other good tools are; journaling, writing three things, writing gratitude list, watching brother David Steindle-Rast's YouTube "A Good Day." I will briefly describe each here. Try them as you work through the process of the Steps to help you along the way. We were using our addictions to cope, these tools are better.

A healthy diet, good rest and moderate exercise also are a great help to getting healthy. You may like to take a good look at these as you begin to treat yourself better.

Ho 'O Ponopono: Ho 'O Ponopono is a Hawaiian healing ceremony that invites practitioners to clear blocked energy, trauma, and wounds converting negative energy into positive energy, love and a deepened interpersonal connection. I have used and found very effective this simplified version. There are times when I am caught up in negative thoughts, ruminating about something I either don't understand or have no control over. Basically, this prayer/chant is requesting it to be "made right"

I start by reciting a short prayer and then repeat over and over four phrases like a chant or mantra. This has been very helpful to clear away negative emotions.

Ho 'O Ponopono

Divine Mother Father and Son, united as one. For all the things I have done, my family has done, my ancestors have done, in this lifetime or in any other, that have caused me to be separate from you: I am truly sorry, please forgive me. And I give thanks for I know it is already so.

I love you
I'm sorry
Forgive me
Thank You

Faster EFT: Have you heard of "Tapping"? Like so many things when I first heard of it I thought it was the silliest thing. Well It has turned out that it really does something that nothing else does quite as well. I think there are emotions held in the body associated with memories. Cellular memory? Tapping seems to help dispel them. There are many books and certification programs with all kinds of formulas and processes. I have found the simplified "Faster EFT" to be enough and have found relief from unpleasant feelings every time I use it. There are You Tubes by Robert G. Smith you may like to check them out.

I read somewhere that research did show improved feelings with tapping anywhere on the upper torso. I picture a fifty-gallon drum full of water. If you tap on the side of it over and over it will set up a vibration that effects the entire drum of water. I guess that is what it does for our body. Emotions that are creating negative feelings can be broken up and released. "let it go"

You start tapping on your eye brow and say, "let it go "then tapping on you temple "let it go", then under your eye on the cheek bone "let it go", then your collar bone "let it go" finally grasping one wrist in your other hand take a deep breath and let it out saying "peace". Repeat several cycles and feel it lighten your feelings. Try it, you'll like it.

While I was watching Robert G. Smith demonstrate this in a video, it occurred to me that the Ho 'O Ponopono four phrases would fit very nicely instead of the "let it go". So, that is how I often do it. Combining them both, Ho 'O Ponopono and Faster EFT.

Laughing Yoga: There are many books and You Tube videos about this also. There are groups that get together every morning and practice together. It's simple really. You can just look in the mirror and start laughing. Fake laughing is okay. Nothing needs to be funny. Keep it up until it becomes real laughing. I have found it is a great antidote for negative thoughts. To actually move my diaphragm in the laugh I think stimulates the vagus nerve disrupting negative emotions. Adding this to the combination of Ho 'O Ponopono and Faster EFT creates a super-fast clearing of negativity. I have made a short You Tube video that describes combining these. At some point you may like to look at it. I would recommend you familiarize yourself with each tool before combining them. My YouTube channel is *www.youtube.com/c/HappyHypnosisSedona* "click" on "videos" to see a short five minute video about combining them. Or follow this link *https://youtu.be/ON1eW6-fnmQ*

Breath work: In the book *The Miracle of Mindfulness* Thich Nhat Hanh describes the benefits of breath work. The breath is kind of like a connection between the conscious and subconscious. Apparently when you focus on your breath you create a calming effect. When you breath out longer than you breath in this has a greater calming effect. So, breath in for a count of seven and out for a count of eleven. Make it comfortable, you can use five and seven or three and five, whatever allows you to focus on your breath, breathing out a little longer than you breath in. There is a six minute MP3 on the home page of my site *www.HappyHypnosisSedona.com.* It's Six Minutes of Mindfulness and it just leads you through mindful breathing. Very calming. A great daily practice.

Journaling: there are parts of our minds, some more confused than others. The part of our mind that deals with language the Broca Center is more advanced and reasoning than the limbic center where emotions exist. When we write about our feelings it brings it out of the emotional limbic center into the reasoning neocortex Broca center. As I understand it, this is why I feel better when I talk about a problem and even better still when I write about it. One of the mistakes many make, and I made myself, is thinking that just thinking about what I'm supposed to be writing, is going to give me the same benefits.

Just thinking it won't bring it through the Broca center like writing about it does.

Gratitude: I often assign my clients the task of writing three things that went well today at the end of the day. I do this myself. Studies have shown people who do this simple practice will be 15% happier! I learned this in a course I took through UC Berkeley, called the Science of Happiness. Great stuff!

Write a gratitude list, always a good thing. Thich Nhat Hanh sometimes starts a talk by saying "today I am grateful for my non-heart attack". Apparently just the act of looking for what you are grateful for will produce an improved mood. There is a great You Tube video by Brother David Steindl-Rast "A good Day". He is all about gratitude. Gratitude is the antidote to all negativity. When I stopped being a victim and started realizing what I am grateful for, it changed everything. That is what the whole point is, my mind is like a radio, to change my radio from the "life sucks channel" to the "good news network" is the path to being Happy Joyous and Free.

CHAPTER 4

The Steps

Here I'll describe my experience, strength, and hope. I want to emphasize I don't think I have any better knowledge of the steps. I just want to describe what I did and what I help sponsees and clients do. I especially want to describe how hypnosis helps the process. There are many guides through the steps. This is not intended to be one of those. Use one of them with a sponsor and use this as an aide/supplement. I highly recommend NA's *The NA Step Working Guides*. I hope you're listening to a hypnosis recording at least daily. There are three I have written intended to help with step one. "Easy does it but DO it", "Done" and "Hypnosis for Step 1".

Step 1

1. **We admitted we were powerless over _____ and our lives had become unmanageable.**

There's a problem with me that I haven't been able to change on my own and it's bad enough that I'm willing to get help with it.

Both times for me I had to be told. It was very unpleasant both times. When I was in my addiction, my addiction was telling me I was okay. Everybody else was wrong.

Most therapists will tell you that just recognizing you have a problem is 90% of the job of fixing it. I have found that until you stop the problem that is disrupting your life it is difficult if not impossible to clean up the underlying issues that are leading you to seek escape.

Addictions are patterns stored in our subconscious. A trigger is pulled, a button is pushed and the pattern is played out. I have heard people describe feeling like they were in the back seat watching themselves carrying out the problem behavior i.e. going to the liquor store, tracking down a dealer, placing a bet..........

For myself as a hypnotherapist I definitely could see the benefit of using hypnosis to interrupt this pattern. That is what the hypnosis I have written "Done" is designed to do. As soon as you're aware you are being triggered you instantly switch your thinking to your bottom. By practicing this while in hypnosis it becomes an automatic program in your subconscious. Like pushing the "record" button on the tape recorder, recording over the old tape and recording a new version. Each time you do it, it weakens that old pattern that was driving your addiction (neuroplastic pruning).

What is your bottom. What makes you realize you have a problem? For me it was being sat down by my wife and her best friend and told. "There's the door, go to AA and get straightened out and maybe we'll talk about you coming back."

So, in hypnosis I rehearse being "triggered" and immediately thinking of how it felt at that moment." Practicing this over and over in hypnosis. Picturing myself in many different situations where in the past I would have _____ then instantly recalling my bottom and how it felt.

This is like Pavlov's dog. Every time you feed the dog you ring a bell. Every time you think of that old problem behavior you remember your bottom. This collapses that old pattern. Synapses actually disconnect in your neuropathways (pruning). When you've done this enough the thought of that old behavior is no longer appealing. This is neuroplasticity.

These problems all reside in the SUBconscious. Hypnosis reaches in there beneath the analytical mind and like pressing "record" on a tape recorder it can erase old patterns and record new healthy ones. (pardon me if I repeat myself)

Are you listening to a hypnosis recording daily? Studies show that people who do have a 26 to 39% more robust immune system.

Any time is a good time. If you listen to one a day that will be great. More is okay but less is not recommended. The repetition is very powerful for rewiring the brain to a healthier "rest and restore" default setting more and more of the time. Always keep an eye out for faulty programming that can be rewired.

One of the great minds involved in the origins of AA was Dr. Silkworth. He noticed a high percentage of alcoholics had a higher than average anxiety level. My studies in hypnosis have led me to believe that all sorts of diseases, mental, physical, or spiritual have common origins in higher than necessary anxiety levels. For most of us, the fight or flight (or freeze) response is being triggered too often.

When I was early in recovery and coming off antidepressant medications I listened to hypnosis recordings three times a day for months. Hopefully you are not as bad off as I was but if you are, that's okay, you will get through this, it will pass like everything else. If you're desperate, talk to people, get help. Use as many hypnosis sessions as you need.

My advice is to find an educated skilled therapist who has personal experience with 12 Steps and non-pharmaceutical solutions, including hypnosis, and discuss your situation with him or her. I am available via Skype to offer customized hypnosis sessions.

This is my second recovery from alcoholism, I have also suffered from depression to the point that I was at the maximum dose of one antidepressant and started on an additional one. In the year 2009 I was on nine different pharmaceuticals, 100 pounds overweight, smoking my pipe like a chimney (tobacco) and severely depressed. Some of the details are like so many you hear at 12-Step meetings.

One definite thing I found often recounted in personal stories at meetings and alluded to by Dr. Silkworth was an underlying self-centered fear and anxiety. For many of us this had been present from birth and really the root cause of so much of our aberrant behavior. The logs in the fire fueling our need for escape.

We were looking for relief from this feeling of not fitting in, something always feeling wrong. I remember telling a therapist in my teens that I never felt good except when high on something. She said that wasn't normal, that I should look into the reasons for that. That's what I have done and you can too. It took me forty years.I wish I had found hypnosis sooner, I wish I never took the prescribed medications that were supposed to fix the so called chemical imbalance in my brain. I can't go back and change my life but I can write a great ending. NA tells us, "We were looking for something and thought we had found it in drugs." You hear so many say their addiction was their solution. Their problem was their thinking. That's the problem programming we're looking to rewire using the steps and hypnosis.

I think good advice is to look for the winners then do what they did. The winners are the ones who seem to enjoy life in a relaxed casual way. A smart guy I once knew said "while it is true not all neurotics are alcoholic, it is also true that all alcoholics ARE neurotic." Addictions are patterns. You get a trigger and out comes this computer program that results in your addictive behavior being played out. A drink, a bet, a romance, a fight, a rage, a theft, whatever behavior it is that you're stuck, repeating over and over seemingly without any choice.

That's the problem we're here to help you get out of. It's not magic, but it seems like it. In a real sense, it's a miracle, the miracle of recovery played out in 12-Step programs all over the world. Until those guys put it into the Big Book there really wasn't any dependable way to help an addict. "Once an addict, always an addict." Like Pavlov's dog hearing a bell every time it's fed until every time it hears a bell it salivates even in the absence of food. Through repetition it has been hardwired into your brain. It's in there so insidiously that you haven't been able to quit it in spite of the fact that consciously you can clearly see that it is causing you misery instead of making life wonderful.

Apparently, there is an invisible line that once you cross over, you can never go back. I guarantee that it gets easier every time you don't pick up. The urge gets weaker and weaker and farther and farther apart until someday it's just a distant memory of something you used to do but you wouldn't do now. This is neuroplasticity in action (pruning). Hypnosis really helps with this. Rehearsing in a hypnotic trance being successful at changing the pattern rewires our brain like pushing record on the tape recorder.

Don't _____ no matter what and keep coming back to the meetings, and working on the Steps. Get lots of phone numbers. A good sponsor will tell a new person to call someone in the program every day and just say "Hi, this is a recovery call. I'm practicing calling people so if I ever have a time when I'm having a problem not picking up I will be more used to calling people." Programing a new helpful pattern.

When you are confident you are convinced you are going to continue to try to adopt this way of life you can shift your attention to the concepts in Step 2. You might like to start listening to "Hypnosis for Step 2" daily adding the previous ones any time you feel you could use reinforcement. The script for it is in Appendix A. Record it for yourself or have someone else do it. Or you can download a recording in my voice at a reasonable price from my website www. HappyHypnosisSedona.com

Step 2

2. Came to believe that a power greater than ourselves could restore us to sanity.

I hate to tell you how complicated this was for me. Like everything in a neurotic's mind, it was all mixed up in mine. On one level I wouldn't be in the rooms if I didn't think there was relief there for me but on the other hand I had to analyze and debate all the implications of this simple concept.

In my life, I have been an Atheist/Methodist, Agnostic, Born again Methodist, Non-denominational, Atheist, Agnostic, Buddhist, Native American Spirituality, Spiritualist, New Age Chakra Nut. I now consider myself a Freethinker. I believe there is a Universal Loving Intelligence that connects us all when we are seeking a higher purpose but that could all change again tomorrow. I heard even Mother Theresa had her doubts. I have come to realize the smartest thing I ever said was "I don't Know."

Self-centered fear and a lack of a sense of a higher power seems to be a common theme with us in need of the 12-Step programs. Something seems to be missing. We try to find relief from this feeling of not being safe, not fitting in, not being worthy. As I heard other people's stories I started to hear things that resonated with me. I also started to hear how there was a solution. They were as lost as I had been and they now seemed comfortable with their lives. Comfortable in their own skin.

Back when I knew everything (my first sobriety), if someone talked about fears of any kind I smugly told them fear is just a lack of faith, give it to God. I guess I had lost my faith in my second recovery. In my first recovery, it was a snap. I was close to being a born again Christian. This second time I was totally convinced there was no God. Or worse, that if there was He was useless, even evil. I had done everything right and it all had gone wrong. Santa Claus had not come through.

Is there a God? If there is, how do I interact with Him? If there isn't and I act as if there was, what will the harm be? The chapter in the Big Book "To the agnostic" really does an incredible job of sorting this out and considers every imaginable problem with this concept. Bottom line, if you concede that the group of people you find in the rooms seems to have found a way to deal with the problem you have completely failed to solve, then there's your Higher Power, the group itself and you can go with that. There are Atheists as well as devout believers in all manner of religions who have found relief from their addictions through the practice of these 12 Steps. Using self-hypnosis is only going to help in rewiring those old patterns and establishing the new ones.

At a certain point in my recovery (around eight months) I was still suffering from depression, I certainly wasn't happy joyous and free. In my first recovery, things had come so easy, that in hindsight I realize the big difference was my acceptance of a Higher Power.

In my first recovery, I had no doubt. In this second recovery, I had nothing but doubt and confusion. And here I was eight months without a drink or drug of any kind and I was miserable, I felt cheated, I was angry and resentful.

A guy said in a meeting regarding Step 2 that he didn't know what his higher power was but he hadn't had a drink or even the desire to drink in 18 years and that that, in itself, was a miracle and proof that there was a Higher Power because on his own he had never been able to go a day without using. That really rang true to me! It was like a light switch had been turned on. I hadn't had a drink in eight months, I hadn't even thought of a drink even though I was miserable, suicidal, homicidal. That was a turning point for me, just one of many but a really big one.

Going to meetings daily exposed me to many examples of miracles in other people's lives. You see that over and over and even the worst skeptic is going to open up. They say in the description of spiritual experiences on page 568 of the Big Book, "Willingness, honesty and open mindedness are the essentials of recovery."It took me 8 months to achieve that but when I did things started to get better fast.

I can recognize something consciously but modern neuropsychology tells us we have two minds. More than 95% of my mind is subconscious, that's where alcoholism and addiction live. The patterns that exist on subconscious levels drove my drinking. Consciously I would plan to have just two and go home. But as I had those two, subconscious patterns were activated that ordered up the third, fourth and on to destruction. Hypnosis allows us to bypass the analytical mind and affect the subconscious patterns below. It's like pushing "record" on a tape recorder and erasing old patterns as we record new healthy ones. (did I say that before? It's worth repeating. I'll probably say it again.)

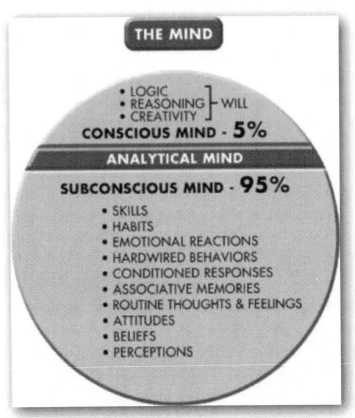

copied from <u>You Are the Placebo</u> by Dr Joe Dispenza.

So why not use hypnosis to break that up? Become a moderate, sane drinker. Well, in The Big Book he says that maybe early in our drinking we could have done that. I have had hypnosis clients who were early in this progression and with just one or two sessions and some sharing of my experience, emphasizing that if they didn't wake up and pay attention they were at a fork in the road. Go much further and you will cross a line if you haven't already.

There is an invisible line. Once you cross it you can't go back. In the video "Alcoholism, the Medical Model" they talk about a chemical found in the brain of alcoholics and heroin addicts alike; THIQ, Tetrahydrosoisoquinoline. Apparently, according to this theory, this substance builds up somewhere in the brain during the active addiction and doesn't dissipate during periods of abstinence. It is produced somewhere in the cycle of obsession and use. Once a cucumber has been made into a pickle, it can never be made back into a cucumber.

This would explain why, when a problem drinker/addict dries out for a long period of time, if he ever picks up again this substance in his brain is activated and his addiction starts right back up where he left off. Hence once an alcoholic always an alcoholic, addict, gambler, whatever.

If you straighten up and fly right early enough in this cycle, identify the underlying angst that is causing your drinking, catch it early enough and start to use responsibly, you can break the pattern and drink like a normal person.

I've had a few clients who have straightened out their subconscious demons and used hypnosis to limit their use and all is well without the whole hit bottom and get to the meetings thing. I have proven beyond a doubt to myself I have been pickled and will never be a cucumber again. I can never safely drink.

I use my experience to help them see they are at a crossroad and if they don't shape up they will go over that invisible line. They will be a pickle. THIQ will have built up in their brains and there is nothing that can be done, if they use they will have trouble, they will have lost any control and will no longer be able to have just one or two. Then they will either adopt a spiritual life and follow the 12 Steps in all their affairs or ride out their addiction to jails, institutions or death leaving a path of destruction and pain for themselves and everyone who loves them.

In order for my patterns to change I had to believe that they could change. Dr. Bruce Lipton PhD. (author of *Biology of Belief*) says (and I would agree) there are really only two ways to change patterns in the subconscious mind. One is through hypnosis and the other through repetition. Hence the 90 meetings in 90 days, the readings of the same material at the beginning of every meeting. How it works over and over. (oops did I say that before!?!)

Bottom line, there is a miracle that can happen for you. Your addiction can be put to sleep, but you have to say "May I," you have to admit you're not the all-powerful wizard of Oz, that you're just another Bozo on the bus and that like everyone else you need help. If you do that the help is there for you. You can obtain a "daily reprieve contingent on your maintenance of your spiritual condition."

If, like me in my first recovery, you hold back a little, and secretly think somewhere inside that you're really the all-powerful but you'll just play the part of a humble servant relying on this "Higher Power," habituation will help you. Not as thoroughly as hypnosis (prayer and meditation) but it will help.

Many people do their own versions of the program and as long as they don't drink they're way better off than they were when drinking. But to be completely happy joyous and free, to have the whole enchilada: "With all the earnestness at our command we beg of you to be fearless and thorough from the very start."

I recently had an experience that bumped my agnostic views up to a Non-Dualistic view. Miracles do happen but my inner self is more involved than I knew. I have heard of "manifesting" and the Power of a Positive Mental Attitude but I was coming back from a severe disillusionment.

So, about what happened, I was at a Dr Joe Dispenza Advanced Workshop in Cabo, MX. He was leading a group of 500 people teaching us to get out of our lower "survival emotions" and into our higher "divine creative." To have things we want to see in our lives happen. He also talks about our turning things over to a Divine Creative Intelligence that loves us. He had talked about our asking for a sign, something that would prove to us there was contact with this intelligence. Something we hadn't expected but would prove it to us. Well I honestly didn't very seriously do that but something happened anyway.

On the next day, he showed an image of the pineal gland alongside an image of the "Eye of Horus" in preparation for a deep meditation to activate the pineal gland.

Copied from the internet, source unknown.

On that very day, I got an email from Armen Ra, a client I had done Skype hypnosis with. He is a world renowned Theraminist and personality extraordinaire. His Movie "When my Sorrow Died" Had shown here in Sedona and I was lucky enough to meet him in person. I offered him a Skype hypnosis session hoping to help him with issues illuminated in the movie and of course possibly advance my hypnosis practice. We did one Skype hypnosis session but I hadn't heard from him in a year. I had hoped to do more Skype hypnosis for him. His Skype image IS THE EYE OF HORUS (also known as "the Eye of Ra") in his email he asked to do more Skype hypnosis.

I hadn't really thought of it or tried to make it happen in over a year. I thought afterwards how these things are a sign that there are more than accidents in operation. I now believe we are all connected. When I saw that image, it reminded me of Armen. I wasn't even consciously aware of it. And my subconscious thinking of Armen must have touched him on some level and he reached out.

We ARE connected, especially when seeking a higher purpose. I wanted to Skype with him to help him. When I am looking to help, I am in touch with the part of me that is the Divine Creator. I think it is like when you see a thousand birds flying and they make a sudden change in direction without any of them bumping into each other. God for me is a murmuration. When we come together in meetings and want to help the one who is sharing some trouble we are activating the Divine Creator frequency. When we get out of ourselves..... whenever two or more are gathered in my name I am there.

Again, this in my conception now and there is no need for anyone else to agree or disagree. Your job is to try to have an open mind, that's all. I've heard it said the required concept for this step is "There is a God and it's not me." I had to resign from the debate club and just "fake it till I make it" or perhaps just "act as if" there's a God and it's not me. There are some very handy tools that can now be used when you've reached this point. A "God Box" is often talked about. If there is a problem that is taking up too much of my energy stewing about it. I can write it on a piece of paper and put it into the God Box. I read that the Pope uses a St Francis box to put his cares in before going to sleep at night. He reports sleeping well thanks to this.

One of my favorite tools of the programs is the Serenity Prayer
God, grant me the serenity to accept the things I cannot change,

Courage to change the things I can,
and the wisdom to know the difference.

When you feel like you've got a handle on this step you might like to start listening to "Hypnosis for Step 3." The script for it is in Appendix A. Record it for yourself or have someone else do it. Or you can purchase my recording at a reasonable price from my website www.HappyHypnosisSedona.com

Step 3

3. Made a decision to turn our will and our lives over to the care of God as we understood him.

For me I had to "fake it till you make it" this doesn't sound right but it worked for me. Like I said earlier, in my first recovery, I had no problem with this, I had a Christian concept of God and it worked very well for me. This time around not so much. This time I was disillusioned. Until that guy said what he did about the miracle of having the compulsion to drink removed I was sure there wasn't a God, I felt like I had been foolish to have ever believed, like I had been sold the Brooklyn Bridge.

But addiction is a spiritual malady, deep in our subconscious. P 45 of the Big Book talks about a lack of power being our problem and developing a relationship and a reliance on a power greater than ourselves could and would help us out if we let it.

I've heard some share that they were worried they'd be required by their new God to shave their head and sell flowers in airports. This hardly ever happens and when it does it turns out fine.

You may feel that I'm talking out of both sides of my mouth, with a forked tongue. That's okay I probably am. Remember I'm writing about my experience and although I'd like to think I understand what happened I know I really don't.

There's a Far Side Cartoon showing a super geek scientist with thick glasses, wild hair, lab coat and pocket protector, at a blackboard covered with scientific equations E=MC2 and everything else you can think of but in the middle among all these scientific symbols the words "then a miracle happens." That's exactly how it is for me and recovery. Sure, science has a lot to say about it. Hypnosis really does give one a huge boost/jump start but bottom line, it takes a miracle and a miracle is there for each and every one who asks for it by following these simple Steps.

There are all kinds of ways to deal with the God thing and you know there are atheists in recovery. For me, to just go ahead and say the prayers and use the meditation acting "as if" there is a God, actually allowed me to learn to deal with life in a healthier way. Some say "fake it 'till you make it."

Even if you don't believe there is a God, if you develop the habit of letting go and letting God you will find a healthier way to deal with life and find a sense of wellbeing that may have eluded you so far. That's probably what caused your disease. In NA they say, "We were looking for something and thought we had found it in drugs." I've also heard "I had a God shaped hole in my soul and I was trying to fill it with drugs."

So, when you are ready to make a decision to give this a chance, you will find a way of living that is happy joyous and free. And you probably won't have to shave your head and sell flowers in the airport. Some recommend you get on your knees, hold hands with your sponsor (best if you can really do it but you can imagine it). Then repeat the following prayer. (out loud with a sponsor, okay so I never actually did this, but I thought about it.) I do use this prayer quite frequently there was a period when I would say it every morning before getting out of bed. No matter what my concept of God may be, if I turn things over and just do the next right thing I am better able to deal with life.

AA THIRD STEP Prayer
Pg. 63 - God, I offer myself to Thee - to build with me and do with me as Thou wilt. Relieve me of the bondage of self, that I may better do Thy will. Take away my difficulties, that victory over them may bear witness to those I would help of Thy Power, Thy Love, and Thy Way of Life. May I do Thy will always!

NA THIRD STEP PRAYER
God, I am now willing to put my life into your care. Align my will with yours. Help me to recognize and carry out your will. Open my heart so that I may become a free and open channel for your love. Take away my fears and doubts, so that I may better demonstrate your presence in my life. May your will, not mine be done.

The minimum required to continue is only the decision to go ahead and try working through the rest of the steps to the best of your ability trying to be honest with yourself, open minded and willing.

When you are ready for this you may like to start listening to the recording "Hypnosis for Step 4" at least once a day.

Step 4

4.   Made a fearless and thorough moral inventory of ourselves.

Like much of "The Program" I didn't do this very thoroughly the first time. I have always been a "C" student doing just what is necessary to get by. It didn't turn out well for me with the steps. There are things read at every meeting. I was going to one every day and heard them read. "With all the earnestness at our command, we beg of you to be fearless and thorough from the very start." p. 58 BB. I'm afraid I heard this and thought, ok sure for you guys but I'm a near genius I get the point.

After about eight months of daily meetings and doing my half-baked version of things I was miserable, angry and suicidal.

I considered my situation and my options. Either I had to really give this a chance or I was done with this life. I didn't get sober to be miserable, I want to find that happy joyous and free life they talk about.

I had heard several people describe similar experiences until they really applied the steps.

So, as Dan F. often said, "I decided to take the steps off the wall and put them into my life." At the same time, I continue to search current literature on neuroplasticity and methods for changing toxic patterns. One of the books I found was *Unlearn Your Pain a 28-day process to reprogram Your Brain* by Howard Schubiner. I found going through this process of listing every memory that included anger/resentment, Guilt/shame, Sadness/grief, this was the fourth step "on steroids" and just what my particular combination of depression and addiction needed.

I actually did do it to the best of my ability being as thorough as possible. I wrote out all the exercises by hand and still have them. I show them to sponsees to show I am not asking them to do anything I haven't done. At the same time, I was continuing using hypnosis recordings two to three times a day. There are over 1000 different recordings and scripts available at the site I have provided a link to on my website www.HappyHypnosisSedona.com on the page "about Don" at the bottom. There is a handy search feature there. As I looked through the possible issues I could use help with they actually started suggesting ones based on my selections. I still use some of them and often record some for my clients. Titles like "Fear and Anxiety", "Improve Mood",

"Accept Things", "Lighten up See the Funny Side" the list goes on and on I probably have used fifty of the 1000 available. Erasing negative patterns and recording positive ones. As a hypnotherapist, I use the search function to find scripts when I come up with a client that has an issue I haven't dealt with. It is great not having to "reinvent the wheel." The scripts are well written and effective. I have never been disappointed. If this sounds over the top well I truly credit them with making the difference for me. Not only did I succeed in weaning myself off antidepressants and alcohol but I cleared away the underlying issues that were fueling my need to self-medicate. The "logs in my fire" were put out one by one.

Deepak Chopra talks about toxic emotions, fear, anger, resentment, shame, and guilt in his "Soul of Healing Meditation.". The benefit of working through Steps 4-9 will be to help clear you of these. The goal is to take an honest look at everything that has gone into getting you to where you are today. It has the quality of the healing powers of confession. There I have found forgiveness to be the doorway that leads to healing. Many great teachers have told us that holding on to anger is toxic. It can become an addiction itself, feeding toxic neurotransmitters throughout our system. When we forgive everyone for everything and adopt a practice of loving kindness we can align ourselves with the infinite divine. I have found this to be the path for healing.

"Until you heal the wounds of your past, you are going to bleed. You can bandage the bleeding with food, with alcohol, with drugs, with work, with cigarettes, with sex; But eventually, it will all ooze through and stain your life.

You must find the strength to open the wounds, stick your hands inside, pull out the core of the pain that is holding you in your past, the memories and make peace with them." - Iyanla Vanzant

A Buddhist Prayer of Forgiveness

If I have harmed anyone in any way either knowingly or unknowingly through my own confusions I ask their forgiveness.

If anyone has harmed me in any way either knowingly or unknowingly through their own confusions I forgive them.

And if there is a situation I am not yet ready to forgive
I forgive myself for that.

For all the ways that I harm myself, negate, doubt, belittle myself,
judge or be unkind to myself through my own confusions
I forgive myself.

To be able to chalk up all my transgressions, all my resentments, all my fears as a part of the past, the "disease" I am putting right, healing. I follow the directions on page 65 in the Big Book adding a fourth column for what was my part in it. I list out everything as far back as I can remember that caused me fear, anger, resentment, guilt, shame. This is the fearless and thorough part. It doesn't pay to skimp here. How badly do you want to become a new, better, happier joyous and free person?

Step 5

5. Admitted to God, to ourselves, and to another human being the exact nature of our wrongs.

Like so much of the program, it's pretty simple but not easy. I skimped on this the first time through and got little benefit. I at least felt I was doing something but I was still doing it my way and still doing half measures. I left major issues out minimizing my problems. I wasn't ready to be honest and probably wasn't capable of being honest even with myself.

Pg. 75 of the Big Book "We thank God from the bottom of our heart that we know Him better."

I would say when I finally did this thoroughly I had what I would describe as a spiritual experience.

I was with a man who had 33 years in the program, we were meeting twice a week to go through the Big Book and go through the program thoroughly cosponsoring each other. My anxiety had been building. "You are as sick as your secrets." I knew I had skimped on my previous efforts and I just decided to tell him the things I thought I would never tell anybody. As I told him what I wanted to do and started telling him the things I was never going to tell anyone, a calm feeling filled me. Everything in the room sort of faded from view and there was only his face in my awareness. After I told him I felt better than I had in years. Maybe ever. I felt like Scrooge must have felt after being visited by the three ghosts and He was running around like a nut being kind to everyone, giving away a goose etc.

They say we're as sick as our secrets. What a good feeling to know that there isn't anything I haven't uncovered and allowed to see the light of the program. To me putting an issue through steps 4-9 is like running something through the laundry.

Step 6

6. Became willing to have God remove these defects of character.

This is where hypnosis really shines. I have written a really great script for this based on concepts from Dr Joe Dispenza's teaching (in Appendix A and my website www.HappyHypnosisSedona.com). According to Dr Bruce Lipton (author of Biology of Belief), there are two main ways to change the subconscious mind (where all the trouble lies); hypnosis and repetition. I like to use both. Neuroscience tells us we are 95-99% operating from subconscious patterns. I think it is safe to say that all our problem behaviors are subconscious patterns that play out over and over again. Our subconscious is like a library of tapes. When they get triggered they play out. In transactional analysis described in the book I'm Okay, You're Okay, Thomas Anthony Harris tells how we can see patterns in our behavior. One person triggering an automatic tape in another that is the voice of their parent's response, or their defiant inner child.

The BB tells us to pause. This lets us respond rather than react. When we react it's likely to be from "parent or child" described in transactional analysis. After pausing we can respond as reasoning adults.

In hypnosis, we can rewrite those tapes and rehearse responding as reasoning adults. This to me is working with our Higher Power in the most direct sense.

There are hundreds of problem behaviors that are addressed by hypnotic scripts. I don't have to sit around and wait for my problems to be removed. I can practice self-hypnosis, listen to guided hypnosis recording for specific issues. Dr Joe Dispenza in his book Breaking the habit of Being yourself, describes exactly this. In hypnotic trance (meditation) you ask a problem behavior to change. Every time you are aware of it (thoughts of doing the old problem behavior) you stop and say to yourself "change, this isn't loving to me." And then turn it over to your Higher Power and ask that this pattern be rewritten into a pattern that is loving to me. This is the theme my "Hypnosis for Steps Six and Seven" uses. A powerful tool for change that I use myself.

I have personally used dozens of different hypnosis recordings for different issues. There are over 1000 downloads and scripts available to choose from. There is a link to them on my website. www.HappyHypnosisSedona.com

click on "About Don" and at the very bottom of the page. I have personally used these downloads for over eight years and continue to be amazed at their effectiveness. I am constantly on the lookout for subconscious patterns or programming that may be causing me difficulty. When I find one I search out a hypnosis recording to help fix it.

But it says we became willing to let God remove.... Well my Higher Power or God as I understand Him is actually a great part of my subconscious mind. That is what makes me automatically do things without thinking. That can be helpful like say blinking when dust is blown in my face or problematic like stamping on the brakes when someone is tailgating me in traffic. Subconscious patterns that fire off automatically can be helpful or problematic. So just like the authors recommended on P 133 of the Big Book, using these are taking advantage of the resources our Higher Power has provided us with.

It reminds me of the story of the very devout believer who was stranded by a flood. The water had risen so high he had to climb up on his roof. His neighbor had a canoe and paddled by saying "Get in I'm paddling to higher ground." The man replied, "no you go ahead I'm okay, God will save me." Well time went by and the water kept rising, he had to climb up to the peak of the roof to stay dry. Then a Sheriff's rescue boat came by and said, "Get in we'll bring you to safety." But the man had faith in his God, "No thanks God is good, I'll wait for him to save me." The water kept rising and he had to get up on his TV antenna to stay dry. A helicopter swooped down with a rope ladder and the man waved it away, "God will save me" he yelled at the helicopter. Well the water kept rising and the man was swept away and drowned. When He got to the pearly gates he was disappointed "I had trust in God, he let me drown." "What are you talking about" St Peter said, "I heard He sent you two boats and a helicopter."

Step 7

7. Humbly asked Him to remove our shortcomings.

So this is doing it. As we practice the program it starts to become automatic that we recognize we have been wrong and we suffered for it. By being honest, open-minded, and willing to consider I may be wrong and I may need help straightening out. My first reaction is usually wrong. That is why they say when angry, pause. My first automatic reaction to most triggers is part of my problem. If I pause it allows me to respond with "soundness of mind." This is the great part of being in the present moment. My conscious reasoning mind can find the healthy response to things that my distorted subconscious would react to in a problematic way.

If things seem to be a pattern that repeatedly causes me trouble I can find a hypnosis download, see a hypnotist or write it out myself in some way I can repeat my desire to change over and over until the problem pattern is erased. We're looking for faulty programming that can be rewired. The hypnosis I wrote "Hypnosis for Steps 6&7" will help do just that. I have helped hundreds of clients and sponsees do this. You may even contact me for Skype or Facetime hypnosis sessions.

Seventh Step Prayer

My Creator, I am now willing that You should have all of me, good and bad. I pray that You now remove from me every single defect of character which stands in the way of my usefulness to you and my fellows. Grant me strength, as I go out from here, to do Your bidding. Amen

Step 8

8. **Made a list of all persons we had harmed and became willing to make amends to then all.**

A woman I admire in the program talks about the "Hedge Test". If you're walking down the street and you see someone coming. If you want to hide behind the hedge to avoid them you probably should have them on you eighth step list.

A couple of years ago there were two weddings in my family. One on the East Coast and one in the Midwest. I would see all the people in my extended family. I am happy to report I passed the "Hedge Test" completely. (with only a minor need to further make amends to my sister.)

Step 9

9. Made direct amends to such people wherever possible, except when to do so would injure them or others.

This is another area where a good sponsor is very helpful. I did this on my own and made some mistakes. I also put off contacting some people and it only delayed my rewards. The following are often called the ninth step promises they are listed pp 83-84 of the
Big Book. They are talking about the ninth step.

"If we are painstaking about this phase of our development, we will be amazed before we are halfway through.
We are going to know a new freedom and a new happiness.
We will not regret the past nor wish to shut the door on it.
We will comprehend the word serenity and we will know peace.
No matter how far down the scale we have gone,
We will see how our experience can benefit others.
That feeling of uselessness and self-pity will disappear.
We will lose interest in selfish things
And gain interest in our fellows.
Self-seeking will slip away.
Our whole attitude and outlook upon life will change.
Fear of people and of economic insecurity will leave us.
We will intuitively know how to handle
Situations which used to baffle us.
We will suddenly realize that God is doing for us
What we could not do for ourselves."
c. 1976AAWS, *Alcoholics Anonymous*, PP 83-84

Again, I did this my own way. I had excuses, procrastination, and rationalization. Anyway, it took me longer. I delayed the gifts of the program unnecessarily. I recommend my sponsees get this done efficiently. I also didn't use a sponsor very much and made some mistakes that could be avoided with a little guidance.

When I got to the point that when I read the promises listed above and I thought "Wow it's true, these have come true for me." That's when I started introducing myself at meetings as a RECOVERED Alcoholic.

Step 10

10. Continued to take personal inventory and when we were wrong promptly admitted it.

This is the keep it up part of the program, steps 1-3 we woke up, 3-6 we cleaned up, 7-9 we made up and now 10-12 we keep it up.

The promises associated with step ten:

1. **And we have ceased fighting anything or anyone even alcohol. (84)**
2. For by this time **sanity will have returned. (84)**
3. **We will seldom be interested in liquor.**
4. **If tempted, we recoil from it as from a hot flame. (84)**
5. **We react sanely and normally,** and we will find that this has happened automatically. **(85)**
6. **We will see that our new attitude toward liquor has been given us without any thought or effort on our part. It just comes! That is the miracle of it. (85)**
7. **We are not fighting it, neither are we avoiding temptation. (85)**
8. **We feel as though we had been placed in a position of neutrality, safe and protected. (85)**
9. We have not even sworn off. Instead, **the problem has been removed. It does not exist for us. (85)**
10. **We are neither cocky nor are we afraid.** That is our experience. That is how we react so long as we keep in fit spiritual condition. **(85)**
11. If we have carefully followed directions, **we have begun to sense the flow of His Spirit into us. (85)**
12. **To some extent we have become God-conscious. (85)**
13. **We have begun to develop this vital six sense. (85)**

I can't wait until the end of the day to do this. I must monitor myself all day every day. Any time I become aware of negative thoughts (metacognition) I consciously laugh and ask to have it change into a positive one. I may even break into the Ho 'O Ponopono, adding the Faster EFT and Laughing Yoga in extreme cases.

Although I have some issue with some of the P. 417 Acceptance thing I do use it for myself.

> "And acceptance is the answer to all my problems today.
> When I am disturbed,
> It is because I find some person, place, thing, situation --
> Some fact of my life -- unacceptable to me,
> And I can find no serenity until I accept
> That person, place, thing, or situation
> As being exactly the way it is supposed to be at this moment.
> Nothing, absolutely nothing happens in God's world by mistake.
> Until I could accept my alcoholism, I could not stay sober;
> Unless I accept life completely on life's terms,
> I cannot be happy.
> I need to concentrate not so much
> On what needs to be changed in the world
> As on what needs to be changed in me and in my attitudes."

I can't accept the idea that nothing happens in god's world by accident. My Higher Power doesn't make things happen but helps me through what does happen. It doesn't matter here what I believe, whatever you believe, learning to accept things is very helpful.

My favorite is the Serenity prayer I have used it over and over until it became second nature (neuroplasticity).

Really if I could have only one thing from the program I would choose the Serenity Prayer:

Serenity Prayer

God, grant me the serenity to accept the things I cannot change,
Courage to change the things I can,
And the wisdom to know the difference.

Step 11

11. Sought through prayer and meditation to improve our conscious contact with God as we understood Him, praying only for knowledge of His will for us and the power to carry that out.

As a Free Thinker, the word God means something different to me than to many. I have more of a Buddhist or Native American feeling of connection with everything (when I'm "with the program.") I absolutely am in favor of saying the many good prayers in the program and out. I truly believe hypnosis is the most direct form of prayer and meditation. My connection to my Higher Power is in my subconscious and self-hypnosis brings me into direct contact. Making my conscious contact with my subconscious........MMMMM THAT is what Hypnosis is all about!!!!!

> One prayer that I used as part of my daily program for a while and found very helpful was the Saint Francis Prayer
> Lord make me an instrument of your peace Where there is hatred,
> Let me sow love;
> Where there is injury, pardon;
> Where there is error, truth;
> Where there is doubt, faith;
> Where there is despair, hope;
> Where there is darkness, light;
> And where there is sadness, Joy.
> O Divine Master grant that I may not so much seek to be consoled
> As to console;
> To be understood, as to understand;
> To be loved, as to love.
> For it is in giving that we receive,
> It is in pardoning that we are pardoned,
> And it is in dying that we are born to eternal life.

At a meeting, someone visiting from out of town described how when his recovery was feeling sort of flat, someone suggested a list of readings from the

BB to start each day for two weeks. This sounded good to me as I was feeling at a flat stage in my recovery.

AA Readings

Step 3 – Prayer - The Big Book – p.63
Step 7 – Prayer - The Big Book – p.76
Step 11 – Prayer - The 12-X12 – p.99
Step 10 - The Big Book -p.84-85
Step 11 - The Big Book -p.85-86
Acceptance - The Big Book -p.417
Resentments - The Big Book -p.552-553

Reading these, every morning for two weeks really did give my recovery a huge boost. Notice the use of repetition? This is getting into my subconscious mind and replacing selfish, self-centered fears with more awareness of loving kindness and altruism.

Some say prayer is talking to God and meditation is listening. Using hypnosis recordings to change problem patterns and strengthen helpful ones fits in there with this step for me.

Step 12

12. Having had a spiritual awakening as the result of these steps, we tried to carry this message to alcoholics and to practice these principles in all our affairs.

Writing this book is part of my twelve-step work, it has been a labor of love. I've been working on this for 2 1/2 years and as I write this I have a deep feeling of love for those who helped me along the way and those who may read this and benefit from it. There is no doubt in my mind that the Twelve Step program has allowed me to be restored to a soundness of mind that no other method could have done. Again, this book is not intended to be a guide to the steps. I feel adding the hypnosis was necessary for me and I think truly an inspired improvement. I truly feel this work is Divinely inspired that is the truth of it. Oh well. It is 12th step work. Passing on what I have found that others may be helped.

I am currently sponsoring several men and women, I go to a meeting most days, I lead the Monday meeting of my home group. It truly is a great way of life. Many of my basic human needs are met through my participation in the program. I feel through the 12 steps and hypnosis I have finally found a way to live a happy joyous and free life.

Pg. 164 of the Big Book "Ask Him in your morning meditation what you can do each day for the man who is still sick. The answers will come IF your own house is in order."

It works, if we work it -- We will die, if we don't.

Easy Does it but Do it

Please don't listen while driving a car or any other activity that requires attention.

Find a place to sit or lie down where you won't be interrupted for 20 minutes or so. Turn off your phone, put out the cat. You are doing something for yourself that will lead to a much better life. Just practicing the kind of relaxation this recording is teaching you to do has been shown to have all kinds of health benefits. You may have heard of the benefits of mindfulness. Well while you focus your attention on this exercise you will receive those benefits. Recognizing there is a problem in your life is often 90% of the job of fixing it. There is nothing that can be wrong that working through this process won't help. In fact, I've never seen anybody go through this that didn't succeed. Taking time to relax, just twenty minutes or so will help everything calm down, help you think more clearly, help your immune system functions better. So, let's give it a try. Don't worry you don't have to try very hard or even try not to try.....

Time to draw a curtain on the day so far.
Now as you look up into your head,
look as far up as you can without straining your eyes too much.
as you look up into your head take a deep breath in and let it out slowly
take another deep breath, notice if your eyes blink that is
hypnosis coming on you
take another deep breath and hold it
hold it
then let it out slowly as you close your eyes and concentrate on sinking
sinking down into the bed or chair
that's it
and you can pay close attention to these words
allowing the words to affect you on many levels
or you can just let them float by like the sound water flowing over
rocks in a stream
because as you listen or not listen there is a part of you
that is apart from the part of you
that will hear what it needs to hear

that is the part I'm talking to now
and you can focus all your attention if you like on your breath
your breath is a gate way to the subconscious
it is a part of the voluntary and involuntary workings
the conscious, hold your breath
or subconscious as you
breath without thinking while you sleep
so as you notice your breath, the gentle
rise and fall of your chest and abdomen
the way the air is a little cooler on the inhale
and you can pay attention to the split second
your inhale becomes an exhale.

It's a kind of letting go.
Science tells us it takes muscles to inhale but to exhale
you just let go
that's it
let go
easy does it
one day at a time
the past is just a memory
let it go
the future only a dream
let it go
all that is real
really
is right now
right now, you're ok
you're safe, comfortable, breathing freely
and you can focus all your attention on sensations in the toes
on your left foot
then your right foot
which is more relaxed
is it the left one that is right
or is the right one left feeling comfortably relaxed
and you may like to imagine a wave of gentle comfort

and relaxation
starting at the very top of your head
and slowly moving down progressively
across your forehead as
you listlessly listen to these words
allow the relaxation to relax all the tiny muscles around your eyes
relaxing them so thoroughly
imagine tiny weights holding them shut
so relaxed, like thy are glued shut
so comfortably relaxed you couldn't open them if you tried.

And you may want to test that now
then just forget your eyes as you let
that relaxation flow down your face
relax your jaw
allow a little space between your teeth
move your tongue to touch the top of your mouth releasing
any tension there
you can gently turn your head right to left
left to right
releasing any tension in your neck and shoulders
as that relaxation moves down through your
shoulders into your upper arms, through your elbow into your forearms
then into those hands
some people notice a gentle tingling in the hands
or a numbness in the hands
and you can allow that relaxation to move up the arms and through the
chest and upper back
relaxing the internal organs
the heart and lungs can relax
each breath bringing the relaxation deeper and further through the body
through the abdomen, the hips the pelvis
into the thighs, through the knees
down into the calves
all the way into the feet, to the tips of the toes
until all of you is so relaxed

so comfortably relaxed
and you can be curious to see what would happen if you repeat to yourself
over and over silently "my hands are warm and heavy"
"my hands are warm and heavy"
and research has shown 95% of subjects actually raise the temperature of
their hands simply by repeating "my hands are warm and heavy"
"my hands and feet are warm and heavy"

All of me feels warm and comfortably heavy
deeper and deeper into such a comfortable state of deep relaxation.
And you know, it's true that
no matter how thoroughly relaxed you may be now,
there are always deeper layers of higher relaxation
that your subconscious mind and body know about
and you can if you like, it's a choice you make to just
imagine yourself going down as I count down from 10 to 1
twice as deep with each number
getting ready now
10, feeling good, feeling fine
as you continue to breathe deeply, you feel yourself
surrender to a deep and perfect relaxation that is filling your body
and it feels so good to just relax....
to just let go
number 9, deeper, and deeper, perfectly safe, perfectly secure
number 8, deeper, deeper, 7, 6, feeling good
5, like a pebble sinking down through clear clean water
deeper, deeper
4....3....2, very deep
and one all the way down
the very basement of your subconscious
and you can picture yourself on a beautiful path, perhaps you feel the crunch
of gravel beneath your feet as in a dream you are drawn along the path
maybe you feel the springy softness of lush grass as you move along the path.

perhaps there's the feel of sun on your skin
or the gentle caress of a warm breeze as you move along the path

maybe you hear the sound of water tumbling over rocks in a nearby stream
or the sound of birds singing
everything about this place is comforting and reassuring.
Up ahead you come to a beautiful garden
there are flowers of every kind, some are your favorites
some you never saw before, beautiful shapes and colors
maybe you hear the gentle buzz of insects floating from flower to flower

maybe you smell the sweet perfume of jasmine or roses
there may be fountains or statues, rocks, and crystals
everything is here for your comfort and reassurance.
And you can find a spot to stretch out and lie down in this healing garden
you become aware that this is here for your comfort and safety
It is always with you really
wherever you go there you are in your inner healing garden.
You can just touch your thumb against your finger and anchor
this feeling of calm and comfort. Any time anywhere you can remind
your body mind and spirit that there is a place like this just by
touching your thumb to your finger.
And you may like to imagine you can float above yourself there
looking down on the you there in that beautiful garden
notice what it is about the you there that lets you know just
how relaxed and safe you feel.
And you can repeat to yourself
"right here, right now, I'm okay"
"right here, right now, I'm okay"
"right here, right now, I'm okay"
touching your thumb to your finger
And you can get the feeling you are on the right path
the path that leads to a happier future.
And you can make a commitment to yourself that you're going to
make some changes, a little at a time
give yourself a chance to improve everything
just taking it easy
easy does it
but do it

....

....

....

That's good

....

....

....

And you can see yourself lying there in your healing garden strong, able,
peaceful, and relaxed
a whole person in every respect. capable of
all the things a whole person should with feelings of love and
self-worth you are getting better, and the better you get, the
better you get at getting better
And any need to punish yourself, for whatever reason and
most of us do, can just go far away from you. It will go so far and
so distant until it will be just like floating on a cloud, just like floating
into the distance. Just like floating so far away and so distant until you can
hardly see it at all. Now make a picture in your mind of a beautiful, white,
fleecy, floating cloud. Just watch the cloud floating into the distance.
Floating so far and so distant until it becomes so small and so insignificant
that you can hardly notice it at all.
You know that one day in the not too distant future seeing
yourself traveling through time
A week from now getting better
A month from now, feeling good
A year from now, all the difficulties of today are in the distant past
Hardly able to remember the things that may seem so difficult now
And see how your life will be simpler when you've made some changes
Little bit by little bit, getting easier
as you become your own best friend
Stop sabotaging your happiness
Easy does it but do it
You can see how the work you did
One day at a time
Letting go
Just for today

Doing the next right thing
Easy does it but do it

That's good. And you can come here as often as you like in the days and weeks ahead. You can look forward to the many small ways and some of the great big ways this can make your life easier.
And in a little while,
when you're ready
with a building anticipation
looking forward to the improved life you will be living
feeling like a kid the night before a big vacation
or when the school bell is about to ring
as I count from 1-5
you can return to the here and now feeling very refreshed and calm at the same time. Feeling good and confident you're on the right path

1, getting ready
2,...........
3, moving those hands and feet
4, almost there
5, eyes open wide awake
time for a good stretch.
Welcome back, and you can go ahead and touch your thumb to your finger and experience that peaceful feeling of calm at the same time as that the excitement of anticipation of making a better life for yourself and those around you.
You can do it.

Hypnosis for Step 1

Please don't listen while driving a car or any other activity that requires attention. Find a place to sit or lie down where you won't be interrupted for 20 minutes or so. Turn off the phone, put out the cat. Just start by focusing your eyes on a spot on the wall or the ceiling a little bit above the horizon while I say a few things about Step 1 and working the Steps.

And what we're here to work on today, is that there is some behavior, some problem that's developed in your life that you feel you're powerless over and that you haven't been able to fix on your own and it's causing you enough trouble in your life so that you're ready to look at some way of getting help with it. Like going to some 12 Step program. And this recording is designed to help you with that.

So, as you focus your eyes on a spot on the wall
I want you to really notice the color, the details
The shape, the texture
And as you focus your attention there
You can notice what happens when you
Notice that you can notice three things
out of the corner of your eyes.
That while you've focused your attention on that one spot
You can see three things in your peripheral vision.
You can just gently let those eyes close
And imagine what it would look like
If you zoomed in really close to that spot.
Like it was right up against your nose, how different that would look.
....
And next I'd like you to notice three things that you can hear in the room.
....
You can hear my voice, perhaps you can hear a wind chime outside,
I can hear the fan in my computer
You may be able to hear yourself breathing.
....
And as you
Focus your attention on your breathing
You can notice the gentle rise and fall of your chest.

As you breathe
Notice the feeling of the air as it passes through your nose or your mouth.
You notice it's a little cooler on the inhale,
A little warmer on the exhale
And the great thing about noticing our breath is that
We can focus on breath or ignore it
But it keeps going for us.
It's been with us from the beginning of our lives and
Will continue to be with us all the way through.
And if you notice that split second when the inhale
becomes an exhale

....

Science tells us it takes effort; it takes a muscular effort to breathe in
but to breathe out is just a release.
As you continue to breath comfortably
You can imagine a gentle relaxation, like a wave of comfort
Starting at the very top of your head and gently
Moving down across your forehead,
Around those eyes
Relaxing all the tiny muscles around those eyes
That's good

....

And every breath you take, can just move that relaxation
Steadily, comfortably across your face.
Relaxing your jaw, allow a little space between your teeth
As your jaw relaxes, each and every breath can gently
Move that relaxation through that neck
Across the shoulders
Through your arms,
All the way into your fingers, the very tips of your fingers
And some people notice a tingling or numbness
In the hands and you can be curious to notice
If one hand is more relaxed than the other
Whether the left hand is the right one to be more relaxed or if it's
The right hand that's left feeling more relaxed
And just allow that relaxation to float up

Through your arms and across your chest and down your upper back
Relaxing the upper torso,
The heart and lungs relaxing, each and every
Breath can just gently move that relaxation
A little deeper, a little further
Across your abdomen, your buttocks
Through your pelvis into your thighs
Across your knees into your calves
Filling your feet with a gentle
Relaxation all the way to the tips of those toes
Till all of you is completely relaxed
....
And you can be curious to notice what would happen if you
Repeated to yourself silently
"My hands are warm and heavy,"
"My feet are warm and heavy"
"My hands and feet are warm and heavy"
And science tells us that 95%
Of subjects can actually raise the temperature of their hands
And feet simply by repeating "my hands and feet are warm and heavy"
And you may notice you're feeling more comfortable and relaxed,
No matter how relaxed you may be now, there are levels
And levels of deeper and more comfortable relaxation
That your subconscious mind knows,
And as I count down from ten to one
You can just allow yourself, it's a choice you make to let go
With each number, twice as relaxed.
Number ten getting ready, feeling good, perfectly safe
Perfectly secure
Number nine, as you continue to breathe deeply
You feel yourself surrender, just let go
To this deep perfect relaxation that's filling your body
And you feel so good,
Number eight
Deeper and deeper
Number seven, twice as deep,

Feeling good, feeling fine
Perfectly safe, perfectly secure
Number six, deeper, and deeper
Number five, very, very deep
Like a pebble, continuously drifting down
Deeper and deeper, through clear water,
Deeper...and deeper
Number four, feeling good, feeling fine
Number three, twice as deep, deeper, and deeper
Number two, very deep
And number one
All the way down, letting your subconscious
Allow you all the way down to this perfect level of complete
Relaxation
And you can imagine yourself on a beautiful pathway
Perhaps moving along the path, you feel the crunch of gravel
beneath your feet.
Or maybe the soft springiness of lush grass....
And as you move along the path you may notice the
Feeling of the sun on your skin or perhaps a breeze,
Maybe there's the sound of birds singing or
The sound of children laughing off in the distance
As you continue along the path
Up ahead you notice a beautiful garden

Statues and fountains, flowers and trees of every kind. Some of your
Favorite flowers or maybe some you've never seen before.
Every size and color and shape, and you notice how comforting
And peaceful this garden seems as you find a place to stretch out and
Lie down and consider how comforting and peaceful it seems,
Everything about this place feels good
And you can just rub your thumb against your finger as you
Ask yourself to really anchor this peaceful feeling in
your subconscious mind
Knowing that this beautiful healing garden
Is always with you, it's always there for you

....

....

And as you enjoy the peaceful feeling of this healing garden, you can
Get up and return again to the path leading to a kind of a park
where you see up ahead
There are several groups of people there
As you're moving along you see the first group of people,
They're not that happy, they're having problems in their life
And you can see they're dealing with a problem they're powerless over
And they're suffering from different kinds of unmanageability,
unmanageability,
that causes them difficulties. And you can recognize that this is the
group of people that you're distancing yourself from.
And as you continue on to the next group of people, you can see that this
Group of people, they're more happy, they're enjoying their life
They look healthy. And you recognize that this group of people are no
Longer affected by that old problem, that old behavior they
were powerless over
And they found unmanageable and they've overcome it and they've
Left it behind and you can notice how you just feel like you
belong in this group.
This group of people who are happy, joyous, and free, they're living life
Without fear of people or economic insecurity
They're happier, and as you join this group of people, you notice
There's another group watching as you join them and you
notice it's your friends
And it's your family that is rooting you on and is really glad to see you
Making this decision to join those people and as you
Continue along your path each step you take along the way
You feel more and more sure, this is where you want to go, this is what you
Want to do, these steps you are taking are leading you to that life
Where you can be happy, joyous, and free.......

And you can just make up your mind right now
Make a commitment to yourself that you are done with that old behavior
And you really are going to do what you need to do to stay on this path

And up ahead there are forks in the road that lead to your
Recovery from that old behavior
Or back to that old behavior, and you know it's up to you
You can see where that other path was leading you
And you can just imagine your life
Weeks from now, months from now, years from now
If you hadn't taken this corrective measure
And stayed on that old path of that problem behavior, where it could have
led you

....

....

And you can really be glad
To make that choice, to choose the right path each time you come to those
forks in the road.
And you can just repeat to yourself, "I'm done, I'm done
with that old behavior."
And every step you take you can feel stronger, feel better
Feel like you're on the right path. You are doing what you can do.
And no matter where you've come from, you can go where you need to go.
It's never too late to start doing things right

....

And you can listen to this recording often and you can continue
On this path noticing how every time you rub your thumb against your finger
You can do that now
You get that feeling of peace and calm and the confidence
And the knowledge that you are on the right path
And you're sure that you're done with that old behavior.
And you can get a picture of yourself in the future with that feeling
of happy joyous
And free, feeling like that old behavior is just a distant memory.

Every step you take is bringing you on that path

....

....

And I'm just going to be quiet for a minute and let you just imagine how it
will feel

And how it will look when that old behavior is just a distant memory.

....

....

....

(Pause1 minute)
That's good
It can feel so good to be done.

And in a little while, not right away
You can begin to return to the room.
Feeling really confident that you've made a choice and you feel
really good about it.
As I count from one to five you can return to the room feeling really
Confident, really good, number one getting ready
Two and three moving those hands and feet
Four, almost there
Five, eyes open,
Good time for a stretch, feeling good.

Done

This recording is designed to help you use self-hypnosis to change a problem behavior or addiction. Please don't listen to this while driving a car or any activity that requires concentration.

So, you've come to a point where you know you have to do something. Something has to change. So here is something you can do, something you can always do. Self hypnosis is something you can always do. It has been proven to reduce pain and inflammation, reduce anxiety, reduce craving, and begin the healing process. Taking time to just relax and let your frazzled nerves rest is something that will help everything in your life improve. No matter how bad things have gotten it is never too late to let them start to improve. Something has to change. You can't write your story over and change the past but you can write a new ending that is better for you and everyone involved.

So, just for now
let's just be quiet
for a little while and rest.
Find a place where you can sit comfortably
Or lie down where you won't be interrupted for a while
Turn off the phone, put the cat out
Breath out, closing the curtain on the day for now
Just let yourself rest
that's it
take twenty minutes or so
to soothe your
frazzled nerves and rest.
That's it
Just let go,
easy does it,
just for now.
And as I count down
from twenty down to one,
you can allow yourself
to relax a little deeper
with each number.

As you gently,
ever so slowly
close and open
those eyes with each number.
20 slowly close,
then gently open,
nothing more important
for now,
19 easy does it,
slowly closing a curtain
on the day,
18 as each and every
breath in can heal,
and each breath out
can relax even more,
17 Taking a little time
to take a break
from time to time
to allow yourself time to heal.
16, and if at any time
it may become a time
when it just feels better
to keep 15 those eyes closed
that's okay too,
as you notice the breath
is a little slower
and 14 ....
it may even feel like
there's a tingling in the toes and fingers
13, deeper and deeper
Into a sweet surrender
as 12 brings you down
deeper and deeper,
feeling more and more relaxed,
deeper and deeper
11 ....even the air around you

can feel relaxed and comforting,
10 as thoughts may come
and go
just let them
9 float through your mind
like clouds floating
across the sky,
8 gently floating
farther and farther away,
7, as you drift deeper
and deeper
into that perfect place
of comfort and peace,
6 deeper and deeper
5 and deeper still,
4 all the way down,
3......
2..........
and all the way down
The tiny muscles around the eyesrelax even more, more and more relaxed
And you can imagine if you choose
That those eyes are just so relaxed, they're so relaxed
You couldn't open them, imagine them so relaxed they're like glued shut
And you can test that, notice how it feels to be so relaxed
Eyes glued shut, and you can just forget about that now
and let yourself gently drift even deeper and deeper
to that perfect relaxation
that allows perfect rest
and super learning......
You know there is something that has to change
and you've come to this place of rest
to allow yourself to help yourself
to recognize
You're done.....
you're so done........
you don't have to live that way anymore.........

you don't ever want to feel
like you felt that day,

....

And there's a path ahead
and it leads to a fork in the road
and there are many forks in the road ahead.
One fork at a time you know what you want to do.
And you can see, and you can become aware of
a large screen
TV floating magically in front of you there
or perhaps off to the side,
And you become aware of the image there on the screen
And it can be very sharp and clear or hazy or perhaps
Even just imagine what it would be like to see that there and to see that you
There on the screen in a situation where in the past you would have chosen
that old behavior.
But now there's a part of you that knows you are done with that now.....
and that part of you lets you know....
in no uncertain terms, you are done.....
you are so done with that old behavior
you don't ever want to feel
like you did that day........
and I'm going to be quiet now for a whole minute while you
in super hypnotic
magic dream time
see yourself
in many many different situations
where in the past that old behavior
would have come up
but that part of you that knows
you are done
that part reminds you,
one minute
(pause one minute)
That's it!
Excellent

And you can just rub your thumb against your finger now to anchor that
feeling of
Hope, strength and mastery over that old behavior.
Any time now in the days and weeks ahead where you have any difficulty
at all you can rub that thumb against that finger and the difficulties will get
weaker and weaker and your resolve can get stronger and stronger. And you
can practice this session often
finding you go deeper each time that you do
and your resolve grows stronger and stronger
And now you can if you want just drift off into a deep restorative sleep
Knowing that when you awaken you will feel strong
Or if you need to you can in just a little while return to your awareness of you
surroundings
The position of your body there and your surroundings
As you return feeling good, feeling confident that you are done
That's good

Hypnosis for Step 2

Please don't listen while driving a car or any other activity that requires your attention to be safe.
"Came to believe that a power greater than ourselves could restore us to sanity"

Now if you would please sit or lay down somewhere comfortable where you won't be interrupted for 20 minutes or so, set your eyes on a spot on the wall or ceiling (some people like to use the spiral on my web page) while I say a few things about the second step. Put out the cat, take some nice deep breaths, prepare to close the curtain on the day for now.

We all come to recovery from different places spiritually. And this recording is designed to help you ease into the program of twelve steps with an open mind and an honest willingness. As we associate with these people recovering from the same old behavior that has been plaguing us we can see that this program is working miracles in their lives. If we are honest, open minded, and willing we will see it could work for us too. No matter what our idea of a higher power may be, here is a group of people who have overcome the same difficulty we have been struggling with and haven't been able to overcome on our own. So why not do what they did? Why not forget anything I think I know and try it their way? For me I was disillusioned with faith and rankled at the word God. I found that was OK, the program, the people, the meetings and the steps, could still work for me if I was honest open minded, and willing. If the word God bothers you the way it did me, try doing what I did. Just simply translate it in your mind to whatever works for you at the time. God could mean the group, the program, even your own subconscious mind connecting to the Group Conscious. When I decided to "fake it 'till you make it"; Acting "as if" There's some all-powerful creator, looking over everything. Then I could start praying and putting things in a "God Box"; these are very helpful things in recovery. Like putting down a heavy load after carrying it for a long time. Start seeing things as my business, other people's business, and God's business. There's a lot less for me to worry about that way. If something seems to be worrying me and I can't think what too do I can write it on a piece of paper and put it in a shoe box labeled God's Box.
So here is a very good prayer to get you started.

The Set-Aside Prayer

"Dear God, please help me to set aside everything I think I know about
myself, my disease, these steps and especially you, so that I may have
an open mind and a new experience with all these things. Please
help me to see the truth. Amen, Aho, and so it is."

So, as you make yourself comfortable finding a position you can
keep without effort, knowing it's okay to reposition for comfort at any time.
Closing the curtain on the day for now.
Keep your thoughts on my words and picture in your mind the things that
I'm going to talk about. Allow my words to affect your mind and your body
freely so that you can experience all the benefits from this exercise
allow it to affect you on many different levels
As you allow your body to relax,
I am now going to count slowly to three,
and I will ask you to do certain things at each number in the count.
Ready now
one: look up, all the way up into your eyebrows
look up in your head as far as you can go without
Straining eyes too much and keep your eyes up there
Keep them still like that
2: and while you keep your eyes up there
close the eyelids slowly............. and take a deep breath
Take a deep breath and hold it.........hold it....... And
3: now relax your eyes, breath out slowly
and at the same time concentrate on the feeling of sinking,
sinking down, sinking comfortably all the way down into the chair
feels so good to sit back, relax
And as you listen to my voice you can allow your body
to become more and more heavy and relaxed, limp and loose and relaxed.
Just let your body go limp and loose, more and more relaxed.

Relax your eyes allow the eyes to be comfortably
Relaxed
Allow your attention to shift to your breath

.

Notice how it has become deeper and slower
When you focus your attention on your breath you just naturally
relax a little deeper
Notice the gentle rise and fall of your chest
Feel the air passing through your nose or mouth....
A little cooler on the inhale
A little warmer on the exhale
See if you can
Notice the split second the in breath becomes an out breath
Science tells us it takes muscles to inhale but to exhale you just let go
So, every breath can allow you to relax just a little deeper
We seldom focus our attention on our breath
We have it with us from the very beginning of our life
And it stays with us faithfully 'till the very end
It's actually both a voluntary and involuntary thing
Take a deep breath and hold it, ,,,,,,hold it
now let it out slowly and feel the relaxation deepen

You can do that any time you want to relax a little deeper
Yogis call it a cleansing breath

Now imagine a gentle wave of relaxation gently moving down your body

relax your forehead
and your jaws
Feel the tension evaporate from your jaws, your teeth,
Separating as the muscles in your jaws
become more relaxed
Relax all the muscles in your face
making your face smooth soft and deeply relaxed the face relaxing more more
relax the muscles in your scalp and forehead allow them to become more and
more smooth ....smooth as the relaxation deepens
as the tension leaves your body you can start letting go of all care
all the concerns of the world as you continue to enjoy deeper
and deeper relaxation you can allow yourself to just drift away

drift far away from all your concerns, worries and simply enjoy this carefree
state of comfort nothing matters all you have to do is listen to my words
keep your thoughts on my words and
allow my words the freedom to affect you in an automatic way
on many different levels just let them
feel your face and jaw spread down your body making every part soft
allow the relaxation to spread, the muscles in the neck comfortable relax
your shoulders
let your shoulders sink down comfortably
the muscles become soft and loose
let the relaxation spill down into your chest
relaxing all the muscles of your chest so you can breathe freely and deeply
freeley and slowly and deeply.

as you continue to let your body go limp and loose
letting go of all your tension you can also let go of all your cares
there's nothing to worry about now nobody to please
you can let all your cares just fade away, far away into the distance as your
body becomes more and more deeply relaxed and you listen comfortably to
my words with every breath you breathe out you can relax even more as you
sink down deeper and deeper into this relaxed state
where nothing bothers you
breathing out rhythmically seems to allow you to dissolve or melt into the chair
the chair is strong it can hold your body safely as you sink deeper and deeper
into this pleasant and relaxing.........
Relax your shoulders.... relax your upper back... and your lower back
Feel the tension disappear from the muscles of your back,
leaving only the comfortable sensation of relaxation
relax the muscles of your stomach, relax your stomach
as your muscles relax you can also relax deep inside if your body
you feel the relaxation spread deep into your body
all your internal organs, every muscle, every fiber, deeply relaxed
that really
allows relaxation to flow through your hips into your thighs
through your knees, relaxing every muscle everything

down into your hands relax
your feet, let your feet relax from your toes
let the relaxation spread up so your legs and your knees
as a feeling of comfort
and you can be curious to notice
as you repeat see yourself "my hands are warm and heavy"
"My hands are warm and heavy"
Research has shown 95% of subjects actually raise the temperature of
their hands simply by repeating to themselves "my hands are warm and
heavy."
So as you find yourself sometimes we relaxed you can just allow yourself to
relax deeper
as I count down from 10 - 1 you can just imagine how it feels
to just drift deeper and deeper into that perfect relaxation
number 10 getting ready, feeling good, feeling fine
perfectly safe, perfectly secure, as you continue to breathe deeply you feel
yourself surrender
to a deep and perfect relaxation that's filling your body
and it feels so good to just let go
number 9 deeper and deeper feeling good, feeling fine, as you continue
breathing freely,
every sound, every sensation, allowing you to rest, more completely now
number 8, like a pebble, drifting down through clear water,
deeper and deeper, feeling good, feeling fine
number 7 deeper, deeper, perfectly safe, perfectly secure
breathing freely
number 6 feeling good, feeling fine, floating deeper
number 5 perfectly safe, perfectly secure
as you continue, to breathe deeply
surrender to that perfect relaxation
number 4 deeper and deeper,
feeling good, perfectly safe,
deeper
and deeper
number 3, that's good, very deep now
number 2 twice as deep, feeling good, feeling fine

and number one   all the way down

....

....

and you can just picture yourself on a beautiful path, perhaps you notice the
crunch of gravel beneath your feet, as you move along the path
or the springy softness of lush grass as you move along
like in a dream it's beautiful with white fluffy clouds
maybe you can hear the sound of birds singing
or the laughter of children off in the distance
As you move along like in a dream on this path
you come to a beautiful garden, there are flowers, trees bushes shrubs
your favorite flowers and some have never seen before
You smell the beautiful smell of flowers in the air
perhaps mixed with the smell of new-mown lawn maybe you can hear the
water in fountains
you see statues and sculptures everything about this place,
comforting, relaxing, reassuring, as you find a place to stretch out and lie
down and
really enjoy this healing garden
you feel the sun as it warms your skin
recognize it's restoring your health, restoring your faith
that somehow if you just let go everything really can be ok
if you just stop fighting everything and everybody
just let it be just for now, just for today, just let go and let God
and you can rub your thumb against your finger right now, do it now and as
you rub your thumb against your finger you can anchor this pleasant, peaceful feeling being in this beautiful healing garden................
that's good and anytime anywhere you're feeling a little less than comfortable you can reassure yourself by rubbing the thumb against the finger and
reminding yourself
that your healing garden is right there
deep in the heart of you at the center of the universe
where you are connected to some Divine spirit
and you don't have to understand how just let thumb against the finger
feeling and just let that feeling flow through you every cell every fiber and
you know there's some promises as you continue with this program going

through the steps if you have the willingness, if you have the open-minded-
ness, if you have the honesty
by the time you get to the 9 step these are the promises

"if we are painstaking about this phase of our development we will be
amazed before we're halfway through
we are going to know a new freedom and a new happiness we will not regret
the past nor wish to shut the door on it
we will comprehend the word serenity and we will know peace
no matter how far down the scale we have gone we will see how our experience can benefit others
that feeling of uselessness and self-pity will disappear
we will lose interest in selfish things and gain interest in our fellows
self-seeking will slip away
our whole attitude and outlook upon life will change
fear of people and of economic insecurity will leave us
we will intuitively know how to handle situations which used to baffle us
we will suddenly realize that God is doing for us what we cannot do for
ourselves.
Are these extravagant promises?
We think not,
they are being fulfilled among Us
sometimes quickly sometimes slowly
they will always materialize if we work for them. "p84-5 BB
and now, in a little while
when you're ready
you can begin to become aware of the room around you
the position of that body there
as I count from one to five, you can reawaken
feeling confident that you're on the right path
easy does it as you, number one get ready
number two, three,
moving those hands and feet
four, five, eyes open, wide awake
a good time for a stretch
welcome back!

Hypnosis for Step 3

Please don't listen while driving a car or any other activity that requires attention.
3) made a decision to turn our will and our lives over to the care of God as
we understand him

As you prepare to listen very closely to these words just Find a place to
stretch out or lie down. fix your eyes on a spot on the wall while you
listen very closely to every word. Allow these words to sink in and each
time that you listen you may perceive them differently. that's okay by the
time you get to this point in your process of recovery the effects
of your old behavior probably have cleared away a little and
you can start to look forward to straightening out the effects it
may have had on your life. Some of the consequences your
behavior has created may still be ahead for you and working this
12-step program can certainly help to deal with that.

So, in Step 2 they were talking about a higher power and now
in step 3 they're talking about God. Well okay that doesn't
bother us because we're ready for that. Because no matter
what our past conceptions or prejudices may have been we
are willing to be honest and open-minded right? If not perhaps
we'll just pray for the willingness to be willing and
Honestly open-minded.

so if you're still not sure about God it does say "as we understand him"
I got hung up on that and I hope you don't have to because I still don't
understand him but whatever, whoever, however, we don't want to let that
slow down our progress. I mean there are atheists and agnostics who
have successfully been a part of 12-step programs for decades and it
works for them. So don't worry if you don't understand him. I think some
of the best people don't and personally when I've been so sure I was right
I've never been as sure that I'm right more than once I found
later I was wrong so let's just, let all that go, let's not get
hung up on it let's just let it be

when one of my early Sponsors said what we need for
step 3 is the decision to go ahead and try this way of life see
what happens when I spend my time working on this program
just for today and it is just for today

again, to simplify the first three steps

I can't
he can
I think I'll let him

So, making the decision to go ahead and work the following steps
with a sponsor going to meetings.

continue to be honest open-minded and willing

so, if you haven't already you can just let those eyes gently close
closing the curtain on the day for now
allowing yourself some time to heal
nothing more important than this for right now
know that, no matter what else, is going on in your life
if you take the time, like this, from time to time to
rest very deeply you'll be more effective
in everything you do
As you listen very closely to these words
allowing the words to the affect you on many levels
spend a little time noticing your breath
feeling the air as it moves
in and out through your nose or mouth
notice the gentle rise and fall of your chest and abdomen
that's good
notice that split second when the inhale turns into an exhale
it takes some muscles to inhale but to exhale you just let go
and it can feel so good to just let go
take a deep breath and hold it for 3 seconds
then let it out, feel it like a deep sigh releasing any stress or tension

. and you can imagine a gentle wave of relaxation
starting at the very top of your head.
gently moving down across your forehead
relaxing your eyes
relaxing all the tiny muscles around those eyes
and you can imagine those eyes so relaxed
as if they're glued shut
or there are tiny weights holding them shut
so relaxed you couldn't even open them if you tried
and you can test that now
and as you just forget about that, you can continue to
allow that relaxation to continue to spread
slowly gently comfortably
across your face
smoothing out the muscles
allow a little space between your teeth
perhaps your chin can
move slightly down
toward your chest.
It can feel so good
to just let your head rock
slowly from side to side
releasing any tension
in the neck and shoulders
and every breath
gently drawing
gently bringing that
relaxation slowly,
gently progressively
relax your shoulders.... relax your upper back... and your lower back
feel the tension disappear from the muscles of your back, leaving only the
comfortable sensation of relaxation
relax the muscles of your stomach, relax your stomach
as your muscles relax you can, also relax, deep inside if your body
you feel the relaxation spread deep into your body all your internal organs,
every muscle,

every fiber, deeply relaxed,
that really
allows relaxation to flow through your hips, into your thighs
through your knees, relaxing every muscle, everything
down into your hands, relax your feet, let your feet relax, from your toes let
the relaxation spread up to your legs, your knees, the feeling of comfort
and you can be curious to notice what happens when
you repeat see yourself "my hands are warm and heavy"
"my hands are warm and heavy"
research has shown 95% of subjects actually raise the temperature of their
hands simply by repeating to themselves "my hands are warm and heavy"
So, as you find yourself sometimes so relaxed you can just allow yourself, to
relax twice as deep with every number, as I count down from 10 to 1 you
can imagine, how it feels to just drift deeper and deeper, into that perfect
relaxation
number 10, getting ready, feeling good, feeling fine,
perfectly safe, perfectly secure, as you continue to breathe deeply, you feel
yourself surrender
to a deep and perfect relaxation that's filling your body and it feels so good to
just let go
number 9, deeper and deeper, feeling good, feeling fine, as you continue
breathing freely every sound every sensation allowing you to rest more completely now
number 8, like a pebble drifting down through clear water, deeper and deeper
feeling good, perfectly safe
number 7, deeper deeper perfectly safe perfectly at peace, breathing freely
number 6, feeling good, feeling fine, floating deeper
number 5, perfectly safe, perfectly secure, as you continue to breathe deeply
surrender to that perfect relaxation
number 4, deeper and deeper feeling good, perfectly safe,
deeper
and deeper
number 3, that's good, very deep now
number 2, twice as deep, feeling good, feeling fine
and number one, all the way down

and you can just picture yourself on a beautiful path perhaps you notice the crunch of gravel beneath your feet................ as you move along the path, or the springy softness of lush grass as you move along the path, like in a dream it's
beautiful with fluffy clouds, maybe you can hear the sound of birds singing or the laughter of children off in the distance, as you move along, like in a dream, on this path, you come to a beautiful garden, there are flowers, and trees, bushes, shrubs, your favorite flowers and some you've never seen before, you smell the beautiful smell of flowers in the air, perhaps mixed with the smell of new-mown lawn, maybe you can hear the water in a fountain, you see statues and sculptures, everything about this place, comforting, relaxing, reassuring, you find a place to stretch out and lie down and just really enjoy this healing garden, perhaps you feel the sun as it warms your skin you recognize it's restoring you,
its restoring your health,
restoring your faith that somehow,
if you just let go, everything really can, be ok,
if you just stop fighting, everything and everybody,
just let it be just for now,
just for today, just let go and let God,
and you can rub your thumb against your finger right now
do it now and as you rub your thumb against your finger you can anchor this pleasant feeling being in this beautiful healing garden
that's good
and anytime, anywhere, you're feeling a little less than comfortable,
you can reassure yourself,
by rubbing your thumb against the finger
and reminding yourself that you're healing garden is right there, deep in the heart of you, at the center of the universe, where you are connected to, some Divine spirit and you don't have to understand how, just let go right now and get the feeling
and just let that feeling flow through you, every cell, every fiber,
and you know it means what you want it to mean.
Open your mind and listen to your heart. Here's something nice a dear friend shared.

NA THIRD STEP PRAYER

God, I am now willing to put my life into your care. Align my will with yours.
Help me to recognize and carry out your will. Open my heart so that I may
become a free and open channel for your love. Take away my fears and
doubts, so that I may better demonstrate your presence in my life. May your
will, not mine be done.

....

....

....

and in a little while,
not right away
but when you're ready
you can return to full awareness feeling calm and safe
and just practice any time
rubbing that thumb against your finger
feeling peace.
and as I count from one to five
you can awaken, feeling good
feeling at peace
number 1, getting ready
2, 3, moving those hands and feet
4, almost there and 5, eyes open wide awake
a good time for a stretch
welcome back

Hypnosis for step 4

Please don't listen while driving a car or any other activity that requires attention.

Now if you would please sit or lay down somewhere comfortable where you won't be interrupted for 20 minutes or so, put out the cat, take some nice deep breaths, prepare to close the curtain on the day for now. Set your eyes on a spot on the wall or ceiling while I say a few things about the fourth step.

It's good to keep in mind the point of doing steps four through nine is to clear away the wreckage of the past. To discover underlying issues that were probably contributing to our addictions.

In the book AS BILL SEES IT, on page. 140, he says:

The moral inventory is a cool examination of the damages that occurred to us during life and a sincere effort to look at them in a true perspective.

This has the effect of taking the ground glass out of us, the emotional substance that still cuts and inhibits.

Remember you're not a bad person getting good; you're a sick person getting well. I like to think of the Buddhist prayer of forgiveness. All the things that went wrong in my life are a direct result of confusion. My confusion or other people's.

Buddhist Prayer of Forgiveness

If I have harmed anyone in any way, either knowingly or unknowingly through my own confusions, I ask their forgiveness.

If anyone has harm me in any way, either knowingly or unknowingly through their own confusions, I forgive them.

And if there is a situation I am not yet ready to forgive, I forgive myself for that.

For all the ways that I harm myself, negate, doubt, belittle myself, judge or be unkind to myself, through my own confusions, I forgive myself.

So, for now
You can just let those eyes close
if you haven't already.
Take a nice deep breath and hold it
Hold it and as you let it out slowly
just focus on the feeling of sinking,
Sinking comfortably down
Focusing on your breath
The sensation of your chest and abdomen
Gently rising and falling
The air passing through your nose or mouth.
A little cooler on the inhale
A little warmer on the exhale.

And you can scan that body
For any place where you may be
Holding stress or tension.
Just breath rest and relaxation
There
Now
Just imagine a gentle wave of relaxation
Starting at the very top of your head
And progressively smoothly

Moving down across your forehead.
Around those eyes
Relaxing all the tiny muscles around those eyes.
....
Gently....progressively...
Moving across that face.
Smoothing out the muscles of that face.
Relaxing that jaw, allow a little space between your teeth
As you jaw relaxes,
you may gently touch your tongue to the roof of your mouth
Maybe gently rock your head side to side
Releasing any tension held in that neck or shoulders

Allow that peaceful wave of relaxation to float
Down through, into your upper arms
Through your elbows,
Into your forearms, all the way
To the tips of those fingers,
Every muscle, every fiber
Relaxing, more and more completely
Some people notice tingling in the hands or a
Gentle numbness
And you can be curious to see if
You can notice if one hand is more relaxed than the other.
Perhaps the left hand is the right one
To be more relaxed
Or maybe it's the right one that's left feeling even more
Comfortable.
And it doesn't matter, nothing matters right now.
Just focus on these words and allow
That relaxation to flow across your chest and down your upper back
As you listlessly listen to these words.
It's a choice you make,
Let it go.......
As that wave of relaxation spreads
Through your upper body, your internal organs,
Every part of you relaxing
More and more completely.
The relaxation flowing through your hips
Into your thighs
Through your knees
Down through your calves
Until all of you is so wonderfully
Relaxed the feeling of freedom
That you achieve
As you just let go........
....
That's right, as all of you becomes perfectly
Relaxed...

And as I count down from ten to one,
As relaxed as you may feel right now
You may choose to allow
Yourself to be twice as relaxed
With each and every number
Number ten, getting ready
Deeper.......and deeper
Feeling good...
Feeling fine....
Number nine
Twice as deep....
Number eight, perfectly safe
Seven....and six.
Drifting down, like a pebble through crystal
Clear water, sinking progressively deeper
Number five, deeper
Number four, twice as deep
Number three
Like a high-speed elevator
Down deeper...
Deeper
Number two, deeper
And number one
Aaalllll the way down
That's right
And you can just picture yourself
On a beautiful pathway
And as you,
like in a dream, move along
This path, you feel yourself
More and more peaceful and hopeful
Each step you take on this path
Leads you to a freedom
From that old behavior
And a freedom from
Those old troubles that seemed to be all entangled in

All kinds of ways and as you move along this path
You may feel the sun on your skin or the caress of a gentle breeze
Perhaps you hear the sound of
Birds singing or laughter of children playing
Off in the distance, and
As you move along the path you become aware
of the scents in the air
Perhaps, new mowed lawn
Or the smell of roses
Or.....the sweet smell of rain in the desert
As you move along this path
You recognize
Everything about this time and this place
Is designed for your comfort and your recovery
As you work these steps of this path
You can be assured that there's
Freedom ahead, as each and every step brings you closer
And closer to that freedom
From that old behavior and up ahead, you come to a beautiful garden
You notice there are flowers of every kind,
Your favorite flowers and some you've never seen before
Different colors and shapes
Perhaps you hear the gentle buzz
Of insects as they're floating from flower to flower
You notice there are fountains and sculptures
Stones and crystals
Trees, bushes, everything about this place feels
Reassuring, comforting
Even the air around you feels comforting
And you find a place to
Stretch out and lie down
Just preparing yourself to let go
Put yourself in the hands of a higher power that
Cares about you and wants to help you
As you allow these programs, these steps
To work in your life as you take it easy

As they say, easy does it but do it!
And you can feel the hope
That freedom lies ahead
And you can feel there is some
Purpose in doing this work

....

And there are promises in the Big Book of AA
pages 83 to 84
They're talking about
As you get through to the ninth step

If we are painstaking about this phase of our development
We'll be amazed before we're halfway through
We're going to know a new freedom
And a new happiness
We will not regret the past nor wish to shut the door on it
We will comprehend the word serenity and
We will know peace
No matter how far down the scale we have gone
We will see how our experience
Can benefit others
That feeling of uselessness and self-pity will disappear
We will lose interest in selfish things
And gain interest in our fellows
Self-seeking will slip away
Our whole attitude and outlook upon life
Will change
Fear of people and of economic insecurity will leave us
We will intuitively know how to handle situations
That used to baffle us.
We will suddenly realize that God is doing for us
What we could not do for ourselves.
Are these extravagant promises?
We think not
They're being fulfilled among us
Sometimes quickly, sometimes slowly

They will always materialize if we work for them.

....

And you can visit this beautiful healing garden
Often as you work through the steps
And you can feel yourself finding more and more hope
As you just for today have a program

....
....
....
....
....
....
....
....
....
....
....

That's good
And in a little while,
Not right away
You can just gently begin to
Become aware of the room around you
And the position of that body
As I count from one to five you can
Awaken feeling refreshed, calm and tranquil
And really knowing that you're on the right path
The path that leads you away from that old behavior
Number one, getting ready
Two, three moving those hands and feet
Four, almost there
And FIVE EYS OPEN WIDE AWAKE

Hypnosis for steps 6&7

Please don't listen while driving a car or any other activity that requires attention.
Find a place to sit or lie down where you won't be interrupted for 20 minutes or so. Turn off your phone, put out the cat. Working through the 12 steps is doing something for yourself that will lead to a much better life. Just practicing the kind of relaxation this recording is teaching you to do has been shown to have all kinds of health benefits. You may have heard of the benefits of mindfulness. Well while you focus your attention on this exercise you will receive those benefits. Working on Steps 6&7 is in many ways the meat of the twelve step program. Most people who are "working a good program" will tell you it is a lifelong process. We are looking for progress not perfection. After having worked steps 4&5 there should be some obvious changes you're going to want to make. This is where hypnosis really shines. Our character defects are in fact subconscious programs that often play spontaneously when certain" triggers" are pulled or buttons pushed. While in hypnosis we can see ourselves in situations where in the past we may have automatically reacted a certain way but now we "pause" and ask it to change. Maybe then as Dr Joe Dispenza teaches in <u>Breaking the Habit of Being Yourself</u> saying to ourselves "change, this is not loving for me." We can then turn the pattern over to our Higher Power and ask that it be turned into a new pattern that IS loving to us. So think of a defect or problem you would like to turn over to your Higher Ppower as we move into the session.

(pause 30 seconds)

....

Now start by making yourself comfortable.
Look up into your head
look as far up as you can without straining your eyes too much
as you look up into your head take a deep breath in and let it out slowly
take another deep breath in, notice if you eyes blink that is hypnosis
coming on you
take another deep breath and hold it
hold it
then let it out slowly as you close your eyes and concentrate on sinking
sinking down into the bed or chair
that's it

and you can pay close attention to these words
allowing the words to affect you on many levels
or you can just let them float by like the sound water flowing over
rocks in a stream
because as you listen or not listen there is a part of you
that is apart from the part of you
that will hear what it needs to hear
that is the part I'm talking to now
and you can focus all your attention if you like on your breath
your breath is a gate way to the subconscious
it is a part of the voluntary and involuntary workings
the conscious, hold your breath
or subconscious as you
breath without thinking while you sleep
so as you notice your breath, the gentle
rise and fall of your chest and abdomen
the way the air is a little cooler on the inhale
and you can pay attention to the split second
your inhale becomes an exhale.

It's a kind of letting go.
Science tells us it takes muscles to inhale but to exhale
you just let go
that's it
let go
and you can focus all your attention on the sensations in the toes
on your left foot
then your right foot
which is more relaxed
is it the left one that is right
or is the right one left feeling comfortably relaxed
and you may like to imagine a wave of gentle comfort
and relaxation
starting at the very top of your head
and slowly moving down progressively
across your forehead as

you listlessly listen to these words
allow the relaxation to relax all the tiny muscles around your eyes
relaxing them so thoroughly
imagine tiny weights holding them shut
so relaxed, like they are glued shut
so comfortably relaxed you couldn't open them if you tried.

And you may want to test that now
then just forget your eyes as you let
that relaxation flow down your face
relax your jaw
allow a little space between your teeth
move your tongue to touch the top of your mouth releasing
any tension there
you can gently turn your head right to left
left to right
releasing any tension in your neck and shoulders
as that relaxation moves down through your
shoulders into your upper arms, through your elbows into your forearms
then into those hands
some people notice a gentle tingling in the hands
or a numbness in the hands
and you can allow that relaxation to move up the arms and
through the chest and upper back
relaxing the internal organs
the heart and lungs can relax
each breath bringing the relaxation deeper and further through the body
through the abdomen, the hips the pelvis
into the thighs, through the knees
down into the calves
all the way into the feet, to the tips of the toes
until all of you is so relaxed
so comfortably relaxed
and you can be curious to see what would happen if you repeat to yourself
over and over silently "my hands are warm and heavy"
"my hands are warm and heavy"

And you know, it's true that
no matter how thoroughly relaxed you may be now,
there are always deeper layers of higher relaxation
that your subconscious mind and body know about
and you can if you like, it's a choice you make to just
imagine yourself going down as I count down from 10 to 1
twice as deep with each number
getting ready now
10, feeling good, feeling fine
as you continue to breathe deeply, you feel yourself
surrender to a deep and perfect relaxation that is filling your body
and it feels so good to just relax....
to just let go
number 9, deeper, deeper, perfectly safe, perfectly secure
number 8, deeper, deeper, 7, 6, feeling good
5, like a pebble sinking down through clear clean water
deeper, deeper
4....3....2, very deep
and one all the way down
the very basement of your subconscious
and you can picture yourself on a beautiful path, perhaps you
feel the crunch of gravel beneath your feet as in a dream
you are drawn along the path
maybe you feel the springy softness of lush grass as you
move along the path.

perhaps there's the feel of sun on your skin
or the gentle caress of a warm breeze as you move along the path
maybe you hear the sound of water tumbling over
rocks in a nearby stream
or the sound of birds singing
everything about this place is comforting and reassuring.
Up ahead you come to a beautiful garden
there are flowers of every kind, some are your favorites
some you never saw before, beautiful shapes and colors
maybe you hear the gentle buzz of insects floating from flower to flower

maybe you smell the sweet perfume of jasmine or roses
there may be fountains or statues, rocks and crystals
everything is here for your comfort and reassurance.
And you can find a spot to stretch out and lie
down in this healing garden
you become aware that this is here for your comfort and safety
And you can become aware of a beautiful looking glass there in
your healing garden.
Just floating straight ahead or off to the side.
And you can become aware of an image there in the looking glass,
it's a video of you there and you can see yourself there in situations
where in the past you may have behaved or reacted a certain way.
'Something that you'd like to change and you can see yourself pausing,
touching your thumb to your finger and saying to yourself
"Change that not loving to me"
then consciously turning that behavior, thought or reaction over
to your Higher Power that Divine Creative Loving Energy
that resides in the center of the universe
deep in the heart of each one of us.
Asking that it be changed into a pattern that is loving to you.
and you can see yourself there in that magic looking glass in
many different
times and places where in the past you may have reacted that
way and now however in each situation you see yourself pausing
and saying "Change, that isn't loving to me." Turning it over each
and every time and I'll be quite for a full minute as you,
in super-fast hypnotic time
see this in all kinds of situations
(pause 45 seconds)

And you can get the feeling you are on the right path
the path that leads to a happier future.
And you can make a commitment to yourself that you're going to make some
changes, a little at a time

give yourself a chance to improve everything
just taking it easy
easy does it
but do it

....

That's good
And you can see yourself lying there in your healing garden strong,
able, peaceful and relaxed
a whole person in every respect. capable of
all the things a whole person should with feelings of love and
self-worth you are getting better, and the better you get, the
better you get at getting better
And any need to punish yourself, for whatever reason and most of
us do, can just go far away from you. It will go so far and so distant
until it will be just like floating on a cloud, just like floating into
the distance. Just like floating so far away and so distant until you
can hardly see it at all. Now make a picture in your mind of a beautiful,
white, fleecy, floating cloud. Just watch the cloud floating into the
distance. Floating so far and so distant until it becomes so small and
so insignificant that you can hardly notice it at all.
You know that one day in the not too distant future seeing
yourself traveling through time
A week from now getting better
A month from now, feeling good
A year from now, seeing yourself reacting in new better ways.
Hardly able to remember the things that may seem so difficult now
And see how your life will be simpler when you've made some changes
Little bit by little bit, getting easier
as you become your own best friend
Stop sabotaging your happiness
Easy does it but do it
You can see how the work you did
One day at a time
Letting go

Just for today
Making changes with the help of your Higher Power
Easy does it but do it

That's good. And you can come here as often as you like in the
days and weeks ahead. You can look forward to the many small
ways and some of the great big ways this can make your life easier.
And in a little while,
when you're ready
as I count from 1-5
you can return to the here and now feeling very refreshed and
calm at the same time. Feeling good and confident
you're on the right path

1, getting ready
2,
3, moving those hands and feet
4, almost there
5, eyes open wide awake
time for a good stretch.
Welcome back, and you can go ahead and touch your thumb to your
finger and experience that peaceful feeling of calm at the same time
as that the excitement of anticipation of making a better life
for yourself and those around you. You are committed to
making changes for the better.

APPENDIX B MORE ABOUT THE HISTORY AND DEVELOPMENT OF THE 12 STEPS

Here is an image of the original 6 steps written by Bill W himself in 1953.

The Six Steps

The Six Step program (which later became AA's Twelve Step program) as it was at that time. The six steps were:

1. Complete deflation (which later became Step 1).
2. Dependence and guidance from a Higher Power (which later became Steps 2,3,6,7 & 11).
3. Moral inventory (which later became Steps 4 & 10).
4. Confession (which later became Step 5).
5. Restitution (which later became Steps 8 & 9).
6. Continued work with other alcoholics (which later became Step 12).

The 6 steps as Bill W. wrote them.

1. Admitted hopeless
2. Got honest with self
3. Got honest with another
4. Made amends
5. Helped others without demand
6. Prayed to God as you understand Him

Bill Wilson's Letter to Dr. Carl Jung, Jan 23, 1961

The below is the text of the letter dated 1/23/61, written by Bill Wilson to the eminent Swiss psychologist & psychiatrist Dr. Carl Gustav Jung. Bill considered it a long overdue note of appreciation for Dr. Jung's contribution to A.A.'s solution for alcoholism. The Big Book refers to part of the story on pages 26 & 27. This letter elicited Dr. Jung's immediate reply.

My dear Dr. Jung:

This letter of great appreciation has been very long overdue. May I first introduce myself as Bill W., a co-founder of the Society of *Alcoholics Anonymous*. Though you have surely heard of us, I doubt if you are aware that a certain conversation you once had with one of your patients, a Mr. Rowland H., back in the early 1930's, did play a critical role in the founding of our Fellowship.

Though Rowland H. has long since passed away, the recollections of his remarkable experience while under treatment by you has definitely become part of AA history. Our remembrance of Rowland H.'s statements about his experience with you is as follows: Having exhausted other means of recovery from his alcoholism, it was about 1931 that he became your patient. I believe he remained under your care for perhaps a year. His admiration for you was boundless, and he left you with a feeling of much confidence. To his great consternation, he soon relapsed into intoxication. Certain that you were his "court of last resort," he again returned to your care. Then followed the conversation between you that was to become the first link in the chain of events that led to the founding of Alcoholics Anonymous. My recollection of his account of that conversation is this: First of all, you frankly told him of his hopelessness, so far as any further medical or psychiatric treatment might be concerned. This candid and humble statement of yours was beyond doubt the first foundation stone upon which our Society has since been built. Coming from you, one he so trusted and admired, the impact upon him was immense. When he then asked you if there was any other hope, you told him that there might be, provided he could become the subject of a spiritual or religious experience - in short, a genuine conversion. You pointed out how such an experience, if brought about, might remotivate him when nothing else could. But you did caution, though, that while such experiences had sometimes brought recovery to alcoholics, they were, nevertheless, comparatively rare. You recommended that he place himself in a religious atmosphere and hope for the best. This I believe was the substance of your advice. Shortly thereafter, Mr. H. joined the Oxford Groups, an evangelical movement then at the height of its success in Europe, and one with which you are doubtless familiar. You will remember their large emphasis upon the principles of self-survey, confession, restitution, and the giving of oneself in service to others. They strongly stressed meditation and prayer. In these surroundings, Rowland H. did find a conversion experience that released him for the time being from his compulsion to drink. Returning to New York, he became very active with the "O.G." here, then led by an Episcopal clergyman, Dr. Samuel Shoemaker. Dr. Shoemaker had been one of the founders of that movement, and his was a powerful personality that carried immense sincerity and conviction. At this time (1932-34) the Oxford Groups had already sobered a number of alcoholics, and Rowland, feeling that he could especially identify with these sufferers, addressed himself to the help of still others. One of these chanced to be an old schoolmate of mine, Edwin T. ("Ebby"). He had been threatened with commitment to an institution, but Mr. H. and another ex-alcoholic "O.G." member procured his parole and helped to bring about his sobriety. Meanwhile, I had run the course of alcoholism and was threatened with commitment myself. Fortunately, I had fallen under the care of a physician - a Dr. William D. Silkworth - who was wonderfully capable of understanding alcoholics. But just as you had given up on Rowland, so had he given me up. It was his theory that alcoholism had two components - an obsession that compelled the sufferer to drink against his will and interest, and some sort of metabolism difficulty which he then called an allergy. The alcoholic's compulsion guaranteed that the alcoholic's drinking would go on, and the allergy made sure that the sufferer would finally deteriorate, go insane, or die. Though I had been one of the few he had thought it possible to help, he was finally obliged to tell me of my hopelessness; I, too, would have to be locked up. To me, this was a shattering blow. Just as Rowland had been made ready for his conversion experience by you, so had my wonderful friend, Dr. Silkworth, prepared me. Hearing of my plight, my friend Edwin T. came to see me at my home where I was drinking. By then, it was November 1934. I had long marked my friend Edwin for a hopeless case. Yet there he was in a very evident state of "release" which could by no means be accounted for by his mere association for a very short time with the Oxford Groups. Yet this obvious state of release, as distinguished from the usual depression, was tremendously convincing. Because he was a kindred sufferer, he could unquestionably communicate with me at great depth. I knew at once I must find an experience like his, or die. Again, I returned to Dr. Silkworth's care where I could be once more sobered and so gain a clearer view of my friend's experience of release, and of Rowland H.'s approach to him. Clear once more of alcohol, I found myself terribly depressed. This seemed to be caused by my inability to gain the slightest faith. Edwin T. again visited me and repeated the simple Oxford Groups' formulas. Soon after he left me I became even more depressed. In utter despair I cried out, "If there be a God, will He show Himself." There immediately came to me an illumination of enormous impact and dimension, something which I have since tried to describe in the book "Alcoholics Anonymous" and in "AA Comes of Age", basic texts which I am sending you. My release from the alcohol obsession was immediate. At once I knew I was a free man. Shortly following my experience, my friend Edwin came to the hospital, bringing me a

copy of William James' "Varieties of Religious Experience". This book gave me the realization that most conversion experiences, whatever their variety, do have a common denominator of ego collapse at depth. The individual faces an impossible dilemma. In my case the dilemma had been created by my compulsive drinking and the deep feeling of hopelessness had been vastly deepened by my doctor. It was deepened still more by my alcoholic friend when he acquainted me with your verdict of hopelessness respecting Rowland H. In the wake of my spiritual experience there came a vision of a society of alcoholics, each identifying with and transmitting his experience to the next - chain style. If each sufferer were to carry the news of the scientific hopelessness of alcoholism to each new prospect, he might be able to lay every newcomer wide open to a transforming spiritual experience. This concept proved to be the foundation of such success as Alcoholics Anonymous has since achieved. This has made conversion experiences - nearly every variety reported by James - available on an almost wholesale basis. Our sustained recoveries over the last quarter century number about 300,000. In America and through the world there are today 8,000 AA groups. So, to you, to Dr. Shoemaker of the Oxford Groups, to William James, and to my own physician, Dr. Silkworth, we of AA owe this tremendous benefaction. As you will now clearly see, this astonishing chain of events actually started long ago in your consulting room, and it was directly founded upon your own humility and deep perception. Very many thoughtful AAs are students of your writings. Because of your conviction that man is something more than intellect, emotion, and two dollars' worth of chemicals, you have especially endeared yourself to us. How our Society grew, developed its Traditions for unity, and structured its functioning will be seen in the texts and pamphlet material that I am sending you. You will also be interested to learn that in addition to the "spiritual experience," many AAs report a great variety of psychic phenomena, the cumulative weight of which is very considerable. Other members have - following their recovery in AA - been much helped by your practitioners. A few have been intrigued by the "I Ching" and your remarkable introduction to that work. Please be certain that your place in the affection, and in the history of the Fellowship, is like no other.
Gratefully yours,
William G. W.
Co-founder Alcoholics Anonymous.

Letter from Dr. Carl Jung to Bill Wilson

Prof. Dr. C. G. Jung Kusnacht-Zurich Seestrasse 228 January 30, 1961
Mr. William G. Wilson Alcoholics Anonymous Box 459 Grand Central Station
New York 17, N.Y.

Dear Mr. Wilson,

Your letter has been very welcome indeed. I had no news from Roland H. anymore and often wondered what has been his fate. Our conversation which he had adequately reported to you had an aspect of which he did not know. The reason, that I could not tell him everything, was that those days I had to be exceedingly careful of what I said. I had found out that I was misunderstood in every possible way. Thus, I was very careful when I talked to Roland H. But what I really thought about, was the result of many experiences with men of his kind. His craving for alcohol was the equivalent on a low level of the spiritual thirst of our being for wholeness, expressed in medieval language: the union with God. How could one formulate such an insight in a language that is not misunderstood in our days? The only right and legitimate way to such an experience is, that it happens to you in reality and it can only happen to you when you walk on a path, which leads you to a higher understanding. You might be led to that goal by an act of grace or through a personal and honest contact with friends, or through a higher education of the mind beyond the confines of mere rationalism. I see from your letter that Roland H. has chosen the second way, which was, under the circumstances, obviously the best one. I am strongly convinced that the evil principle prevailing in this world, leads the unrecognized spiritual need into perdition, if it is not counteracted either by a real religious insight or by the protective wall of human community. An ordinary man, not protected by an action from above and isolated in society cannot resist the power of evil, which is called very aptly the Devil. But the use of such words arouses so many mistakes that one can only keep aloof from them as much as possible. These are the reasons why I could not give a full and sufficient explanation to Roland H. but I am risking it with you because I conclude from your very decent and honest letter, that you have acquired a point of view above the misleading platitudes, one usually hears about alcoholism. You see, Alcohol in Latin is "spiritus" and you use the same word for the highest religious experience as well as for the most depraving poison. The helpful formula therefore is: spiritus contra spiritum. Thanking you again for your kind letter. I remain yours sincerely, C.G. Jung "As the heart panteth after the water brooks, so panteth my soul after thee, O God." (Psalm 42:1)

APPENDIX C ALTERNATIVE VERSIONS OF THE 12 STEPS

12 suggestions

"To some of us, the idea of substituting 'good' for 'God' in the Twelve Steps will seem like a watering down of AA's message. But here we must remember that AA's Steps are suggestions only. A belief in them, as they stand, is not at all a requirement for membership among us. This liberty has made AA available to thousands who never would have tried at all had we insisted on the Twelve Steps just as written." ~Bill Wilson "Alcoholics Anonymous Come of Age" page 81. Published in 1957

Secular 12 Steps

1. We admitted we were powerless over alcohol – that our lives had become unmanageable.
2. Came to accept and to understand that we needed strengths beyond our awareness and resources to restore us to sanity.
3. Made a decision to turn our will and our lives over to the care of the A.A. program.
4. Made a searching and fearless moral inventory of ourselves.
5. Admitted to ourselves without reservation, and to another human being, the exact nature of our wrongs.
6. Were ready to accept help in letting go of all our defects of character.
7. Humbly sought to have our shortcomings removed.
8. Made a list of all persons we had harmed and became willing to make amends to them all.
9. Made direct amends to such people wherever possible, except when to do so would injure them or others.
10. Continued to take personal inventory, and when we were wrong promptly admitted it.
11. Sought through mindful inquiry and meditation to improve our spiritual awareness, seeking only for knowledge of our rightful path in life and the power to carry that out.
12. Having had a spiritual awakening as the result of these steps, we tried to carry this message to alcoholics and to practice these principles in all our affairs.

The 12 steps in plain English

1. Alcohol will kill me.
2. There's a power that wants me to live.
3. Do I want to live or die? (if you want to die, stop here)
4. Write about how I got to where I am.
5. Tell another person all about me (let God listen).
6. Want to change.
7. Ask a power greater than me to help me change.
8. Write down who I've hurt.
9. Fix what I can without hurting anyone else.
10. Accept that I'm human and will screw up. Fix it immediately.
11. Ask a power greater than me to show me how to live.
12. Keep doing 1 through 11 and pass it on.

The following is copied from a website soberbastatard.com (asterisks added)

THE 12 F*CKED STEPS

By TheBastard | September 16, 2014 |

A lot of people find 12 Steps programs hard to relate to- especially for non-religious and younger generations. I did not come up with this nor can I take credit for it but I do wholeheartedly endorse it. I present to you- the 12 F*cked Steps.

Step 1: I'm f*cked
Step 2: There might be a way out of this f*cking mess
Step 3: Decide to level the f*ck up
Step 4: Take a good hard look at how f*cked up I am
Step 5: Tell someone else about all the f*cked up stuff I've been through
Step 6: Prepare to stop being such a f*ck up
Step 7: Try to stop acting so f*cked up
Step 8: Make a list of everyone I f*cked over
Step 9: Swallow my f*cking pride and tell them I really f*cked up, except when doing so would f*ck them harder.
Step 10: Keep an eye on my f*cked up thinking and behavior
Step 11: Chill the f*ck out sometimes
Step 12: Help the next poor f*cker that walks through the door

Made in the USA
Columbia, SC
21 December 2017